RESEARCH
ON
CHILDREN

Medical Imperatives,
Ethical Quandaries,
and Legal Constraints

RESEARCH ON CHILDREN

Medical Imperatives, Ethical Quandaries, and Legal Constraints

Edited by

Jan van Eys, M.D., Ph.D.

Pediatrician, Professor of Pediatrics,
and Head of the Department of Pediatrics
The University of Texas System Cancer Center
M. D. Anderson Hospital and Tumor Institute
Houston, Texas

Photographs by
LaNetta Collier

University Park Press
Baltimore • London • Tokyo

UNIVERSITY PARK PRESS
International Publishers in Science and Medicine
233 East Redwood Street
Baltimore, Maryland 21202

Copyright © 1978 by University Park Press

Typeset by American Graphic Arts Corporation.
Manufactured in the United States of America by
Universal Lithographers, Inc.,
and The Optic Bindery Incorported.

Proceedings of the conference, Research on Children: Medical Imperatives,
Ethical Quandaries, and Legal Constraints, held at Houston, Texas on
April 29 and 30, 1977.

Sponsored by the University of Texas System Cancer Center, the Institute
of Religion, and the University of Texas Health Science Center in
Houston.

Library of Congress Cataloging in Publication Data

Main entry under title:

Research on children.

    Proceedings of a workshop held at Houston, Tex. Apr. 29–30, 1977,
which was sponsored by the University of Texas System Cancer Center,
the Institute of Religion, and the University of Texas Health Science
Center in Houston.
    1. Pediatric research — Moral and religious aspects — Congresses.
2. Human experimentation in medicine — Congresses.   3. Pediatrics —
Law and Legislation — United States — Congresses.   4. Children — Law —
United States — Congresses.

I. Van Eys, Jan.   II. University of Texas System. Cancer Center.   III.
Institute of Religion, Houston, Tex.   IV. University of Texas Health
Science Center at Houston.
RJ85.R47   618.9 2 00072   77–25235
ISBN 0-8391-1191-6

Contents

Contributors vii
Preface
    Jan van Eys ix
Acknowledgments xi
Introduction
    Robert C. Hickey xiii

THE RIGHTS OF THE CHILD

Introduction of the Keynote Speaker
    Jan van Eys 3
The Right of Children to Informed Consent
    John Holt 5

THE MEDICAL IMPERATIVE

The Medical Dimensions of Research on Children —
    An Introduction
       H. Grant Taylor 19
Therapeutic Research as a Necessary Mode of Management
    Wataru W. Sutow 21
Children as Therapeutic Orphans
    Margaret P. Sullivan 27
The Importance of Research on Children —
    A Geneticist's View
       Rodney R. Howell 33
The Human as Experimental Animal —
    Necessary or Desirable?
       Jan van Eys 39

ETHICAL QUANDARIES

Moral and Spiritual Aspects of Research on Children —
    An Introduction
       Hyman J. Schachtel 55
Ethical Dimensions of Research on Children
    Paul Ramsey 57
Central Themes in the Debate over Involvement of
Infants and Children in Biomedical Research —
    A Critical Examination
       William G. Bartholome 69
Lazarus Revisited — Moral and Spiritual Aspects of
Experimental Therapeutics with Children
    Kenneth Vaux 77

Discussing the Ethics of Research with Children
    Jerome Berryman 85

LEGAL AND SOCIETAL CONSTRAINTS

The Legal Dimensions of Research on Children —
An Introduction
    Leonard L. Riskin 105
Children as Subjects for Medical Experimentation
    Charles Fried 107
The Impact of Federal Regulations Governing
Experimentation on Medical Malpractice Law
    Catherine Damme 117
Federal Regulations — Their Growth and Intent
    Martha M. Freeman 125
The Federal Government and Policy Decisions Involving
Children
    Floyd A. Norman 133

THE INTEGRATION OF THE PROBLEM

Five Central Concerns in Research on Children —
Summarizing Dialogue and Adversity
    Robert J. Comiskey 141

EPILOGUE

The Problems of Ethical Research and the Problems
with Being a Child
    Jan van Eys 147

INDEX 151

Contributors

William G. Bartholome, MTS, M.Div., Assistant Professor of Pediatirics, Department of Pediatrics, The University of Texas School of Medicine, Houston, Texas

Jerome Berryman, M.Div., J.D., Senior Teaching Fellow, The Institute of Religion, Houston, Texas

Robert J. Comiskey, Ph.D., Postdoctoral Resident in Medical Ethics, The Institute of Religion, Houston, Texas

Catherine Damme, LL.B., Senior Research Associate, Genetics Center, Graduate School of Biomedical Sciences, The University of Texas Health Science Center, Houston, Texas

Martha M. Freeman, M.D., Assistant for Pediatric Drugs to Associate Director for New Drug Evaluation, Bureau of Drugs, Food and Drug Administration, Washington, D.C.

Charles Fried, LL.B., Professor of Law, Law School of Harvard University, Cambridge, Massachusetts

Robert C. Hickey, M.D., Executive Vice President, The University of Texas System Cancer Center M. D. Anderson Hospital and Tumor Institute, Houston, Texas

John Holt, Lecturer and Author, President, Holt Associates, Boston, Massachusetts

Rodney R. Howell, M.D., Professor of Pediatrics and Chairman of the Department of Pediatrics, The University of Texas School of Medicine, Houston, Texas

Floyd A. Norman, M.D., Regional Health Administrator, Public Health Service, Dallas, Texas

Paul Ramsey, Ph.D., Professor of Theological Ethics, Princeton University, Princeton, New Jersey

Leonard L. Riskin, J.D., LL.M., Associate Professor of Law, The University of Houston Bates College of Law, Houston, Texas

Hyman J. Schachtel, Ph.D., Congregation Beth Israel, Houston, Texas

Margaret P. Sullivan, M.D., Pediatrician and Professor of Pediatrics, Department of Pediatrics, The University of Texas System Cancer Center M. D. Anderson Hospital and Tumor Institute, Houston, Texas

Wataru W. Sutow, M.D., Pediatrician and Professor of Pediatrics, Department of Pediatrics, The University of Texas System Cancer Center M. D. Anderson Hospital and Tumor Institute, Houston, Texas

H. Grant Taylor, M.D., Professor of Pediatrics Emeritus, Past Chairman, Department of Pediatrics, The University of Texas System Cancer Center M. D. Anderson Hospital and Tumor Institute, Houston, Texas

Jan van Eys, M.D., Ph.D., Pediatrician, Professor of Pediatrics, and Head of the Department of Pediatrics, The University of Texas System Cancer Center M. D. Anderson Hospital and Tumor Institute, Houston, Texas

Kenneth Vaux, Th.D., Professor of Theology and Ethics, The Institute of Religion, Houston, Texas

Preface

Children are not just small adults. They are different biologically because they still have the capacity for physical growth and maturation. That quality makes treatment of their diseases often easier than treatment of the same diseases in adults. A child will bounce out of bed after major surgery before an adult would dream of moving except with extreme caution. This difference was brought home forcefully to me when I recommended a splenectomy in a father and his 9-year-old son for hereditary spherocytosis. They were operated upon the same day and shared a hospital room at the suggestion of the father. The son was up and active within 24 hours, so the father felt compelled to be active, too. That man suffered a great deal of agony. Children also tolerate toxic agents better. Cancer chemotherapy is much more effective in children because the therapeutic margin is much greater.

But this physiologic promise of growth and maturation is coupled with an inexperience with, and therefore vulnerability to, the sickness-inducing agents in our environment. There are specific childhood diseases that require specific action. Some, such as measles and mumps, are relatively minor, although serious complicatons can arise. More seriously, cancers in childhood can be qualitatively and quantitatively different. Acute lymphocytic leukemia of childhood is a special disease. Neuroblastoma and Wilms' tumor are rarely found outside the pediatric age range. The most severe congenital and genetic diseases, which are barely compatible with life, are seen only in children. All genetic diseases can and should be diagnosed in childhood.

Pediatrics is a special brand of medicine, even on physiological grounds. Therefore, if scientific medicine is a valid approach to solving medical problems, we must conduct research on children in order to remove the scourge of childhood diseases.

But children are not just biologically unique. They must also grow mentally. They need to acquire all the concepts of communication, abstraction, and socialization that will make them functional adults. The young child does not think like an adult and we adults are only too aware of that. We accept the developmental steps as they have been described by Piaget and the self-realization stages as they have been analyzed by Erikson; but we use these steps to prove the child is incapable of communicating with adults and unable to accept adult concerns. We therefore have difficulty reconciling the need for research with the ethical prohibition against conducting research on captive subjects. Suffering from disease is a reality and the child is a poignant patient. Suffering from intervention is always a possibility and we do not want to compound our anxieties about the child. The ethics of research on children are very different from those of research on adults or antenatal research.

Children are also citizens of society. They are the world's most precious resource, but they are also a societal dependence and liability, rather than an economic asset. To use an economic metaphor, children are growth issues, not income-yielding stock. As a society we probably do not like children very much. This may even be true for individual parents. When Ann Landers surveyed her readers, more than 70% indicated they would not have children if they had a chance to start their lives over again. We demonstrate that dislike: children must be protected, but they cannot participate. We do to children on a grand scale what we recently have done to dying patients. We can to a degree describe the stages of dying, as Kübler-Ross has done so effectively. However, now patients are expected to follow that progression, on pain of being declared maladjusted. In the same way we describe the stages of child development, first to excuse our lack of communication and then to force the child's development into the mold of adult society. Of course, children in their innocence do little to impede our efforts; all they want to be is grown up. Nevertheless, we ask children to adjust to our perspectives, and we give them precious little opportunity to be themselves.

Children are a special minority that has rights in our society. Yet we express our recognition of their vulnerability in a patronizing protection. That adult attitude further complicates the morass of regulations, opinions, and responsibilities surrounding research in children. All of us who care for children must be aware of our own reasons for feeling as we do about this subject.

The workshop from which the following proceedings have been taken was not meant to provide information for the national commission charged with writing guidelines for experimentation in children. It was directed instead at those who actually deal with children who might be subjects of research. The distinction between therapeutic and nontherapeutic research was often raised, but only in the extreme is that distinction real. Little research is exclusively for the benefit of the patient. If we knew that it was, no research would be needed. On the other hand, no research is totally devoid of human benefit, for that could not be tolerated. Therefore, the distinction is useful only as a whetstone on which concepts can be sharpened. However, we should never delude ourselves about whether or not the research will yield new data, if the projected medical intervention can indeed properly be called research. And the kind of information to be gained from the data cannot be guaranteed. It cannot be assumed that the information will be worth the cost to the patient.

This workshop dealt with the medical imperatives, the ethical quandaries, and the legal and societal constraints. The participants argued, said things considered outrageous by some. We were caught short by our tendency to pronounce ponderous platitudes and we were surprised by the flashes of humanity that illuminated our professional fiefdoms. We had a good and refreshing time. The proceedings of this conference are now published. Seeing print is not hearing words, but it is the next best thing. Those in attendance were doctors, psychologists, nurses, chaplains, parents, lawyers, government employees, educators, and students. This book is an attempt to share our communication with those who protect all children by caring for that one child now in their charge.

Jan van Eys

Acknowledgments

This workshop filled a much felt need in our therapeutic community. The dedication of the planners, the enthusiasm of the participants, and the willing labor of the supportive personnel made it a success. However, no amount of enthusiasm, work, or dedication would have sufficed without financial support. We want to especially acknowledge the generous assistance of Mr. and Mrs. E. Scurlock, Rockwell Brothers Endowment, Inc., Mustang Tractor and Equipment Co., and Allied Banks of Texas. Their help will have a prolonged impact on the total pediatric care community, and will be translated into a greater understanding of the child as a participant in care and research.

Diane Culhane patiently edited the manuscripts. Her efforts to generate a uniform style without sacrificing the individual authors' special flavor deserve high praise.

As was the case last year, the support of the M. D. Anderson Administration and the encouragement of the Institute of Religion made this workshop a reality. As long as concerns about the child can be so freely expressed in dialogue, there is great hope for the future.

Workshop Introduction

It is a pleasure to come over here to welcome you and to open this multi-disciplinary workshop on research in children, which I think is unique. This workshop is sponsored by The University of Texas System Cancer Center, the Institute of Religion, and The University of Texas Health Science Center in Houston, in particular its genetics center, which is a multidisciplinary group, and its medical school. All of these institutions together directed their attention to this very important topic. I think that those who made up the committee organizing this deserve a special word of thinks — Chairmen Jan van Eys and Rodney Howell, William Bartholome, Catherine Damme, Kenneth Vaux, and Robert Comiskey.

I have read the program of this workshop very carefully. It is intriguing, and it makes one curious. I believe those who participate will be greatly enriched; and when your proceedings are published, I think they will be a source of enrichment for those who read them. But I think the children to whom our attention is being directed will benefit most of all. Dr. van Eys, thank you very much for permitting me to come over.

Robert C. Hickey

RESEARCH
ON
CHILDREN

Medical Imperatives,
Ethical Quandaries,
and Legal Constraints

THE RIGHTS OF THE CHILD

INTRODUCTION OF THE KEYNOTE SPEAKER

Jan van Eys

We have come together here to express our interest in children. The Department of Pediatrics at M. D. Anderson Hospital and Tumor Institute is dedicated to the total care of children with cancer; physical cure if possible, but total care at all times. Because the sick child is not just a disease, our care must involve more than management of the cancer. The cancer affects the child's whole being; he would not be the same child without that cancer.

We, as a group, have dedicated ourselves to this total care, and have made our first faltering steps toward a therapeutic community. These efforts have awakened a new awareness of the human role and personal interactions that total care can give. We now see the person the child can be, but we have thereby awakened new emotions. We have also begun to question our roles, and we are frightened by the captive position in which a child faced with a life-threatening disease is placed. We tend to react protectively, to transform the therapeutic community into a protective community.

One of the first questions we confront involves the use of research in caring for our children, whether our research is "for the patient or on the patient" (*1*).

In a therapeutic community the medical care must be impeccable. The primary reason children come to us is to ask us to cure their cancer. Because we are not sure how to do it, we try to devise ever better ways. We create an environment in which experimental therapy is the best therapy. But there is a danger that the experiment, not the child, may become our concern. That is no more acceptable than rejecting research in the belief that the child would only be a subject of the experiment, not a participant in the cure.

Therefore, we are holding this workshop. We need to conduct research, but ethical considerations should temper our academic zeal, and a social conscience must restrict our actions and protect our charges.

Even in this conference, as child-related as it is, we could easily forget that the reward we should seek is not the cure, but the cured child. Children should be participants whose voices we are trained to hear, not objects whose protestations we are conditioned to ignore. They have rights as patients. We have an obligation to listen to their point of view, but they cannot always speak for themselves. We have taken the next best course and invited Dr. John Holt to be our keynote speaker. John Holt has for many years considered the position of children in our society. His first book was the widely heralded *How Children Fail*, (2), but he has progressed to wider concerns in *Freedom and Beyond* (3) and *Escape from Childhood* (4).

It is appropriate that we start this workshop with an articulate spokesman for children. Children do not always understand what we are doing and we can so easily forget that they should be able to direct their own lives to the best of their abilities. Dr. Holt has demonstrated his willingness to try to talk for the children. It gives me great pleasure to introduce Dr. John Holt.

REFERENCES

1. Richie, E. 1977. Biomedical research: For the patient or on the patient? In: J. van Eys (ed.), The Truly Cured Child, pp. 27–37. University Park Press, Baltimore.
2. Holt, J. 1964. How Children Fail. Pitman Publishing Corporation, Belmont, California.
3. Holt, J. 1974. Freedom and Beyond. E. P. Dutton & Company Inc., New York.
4. Holt, J. 1974. Escape from Childhood. E. P. Dutton & Company Inc., New York.

THE RIGHT OF CHILDREN TO INFORMED CONSENT

John Holt

I want to begin with, but not spend very much time on, the argument that the search for truth, knowledge, and so forth overrides other considerations; that research is per se an overriding concern, that it takes precedence over other values, even though they may be important. It is sometimes said that there should be no restraints or limitations on the rights of scientists to inquire. I do not want to spend very much time on this issue because I do not think it is really germane. The very existence of this conference indicates that many are, at the very least, uneasy about that view. I only want to say, to make myself clear, that I do not believe in it. I think that scientists in any field are, must be, and must make themselves, as much as anyone can, responsible for the effects of what they do. They must ask themselves to what their research will lead. The idea of science as a neutral activity is one that I personally cannot endorse.

In the field in which I am most able to compare what I learned from my own experience with the results of research (the field of psychology as it relates to learning), almost all the direct research on children that I know of is redundant, that is, it tells us no more than what astute or sympathetic observers would see, and have seen, for themselves. The psychological researchers are constantly discovering "wheels" that intelligent mothers have known for centuries or millennia; babies are observant, or things like that. For the most part, psychological research is trivial, misleading, or downright harmful. On my own list of great books about children, only one, a book called *Dibbs: In Search of Self*, has been written by a psychologist or a psychiatrist (*1*). Much insight can be gained from common sense.

My very strong feeling is that, in general, research of any kind should not be done on people without their informed consent. Before

5

amplifying and qualifying that, let me say that informed consent in the area of medicine does not seem to me to be simply a concession to some idea of justice. It is far more than that. It is sound medical practice. There is an old medical maxim, which actually is usually said in Latin: "The doctor treats, nature cures." However, I think it would be more accurate to say that the patient cures. The model of the passive client—accepting, unquestioning, docile, obedient—seems to me as wrong in medicine as it is in teaching, or, I could add, psychology or psychiatry. I think it would be more accurate to say that doctors, if they are to do their work, must find as many ways as possible to ally themselves with the health-giving and health-seeking forces within the patient. It is kind of a truism, and maybe by now for doctors a rather boring and irritating cliché (and if so I apologize in advance for saying it), that organized medicine has not been much interested in health, but very much interested in disease, which is by no means the opposite of health. Health is an elusive but important and central concept. Therefore, the idea of the doctor as the assistant, the supporter, of the health-seeking patient is really more accurate and closer to the truth than that of the patient as the ally of the doctor; that is the wrong way around.

Thus the general concept needs to be stated: as the learner should be at the center of learning, so should the patient be at the center of his healing. Neither the learner nor the patient should be a passive spectator on whom teachers or doctors work their miracles. In medicine, as in teaching, the patient should as much as possible be allowed, helped, and encouraged to know the available options and to make choices. Personally, I would never have any dealings with a doctor(s) or a medical institution that did not treat me that way. I will not submit to any kind of mystification; "we know best," or "you do not understand," etc.

There is one other item I must discuss before amplifying some of these ideas. I would like to submit a famous legal maxim: hard cases make bad law. It is very unwise to try to formulate general rules of conduct or procedure by using as an example the most extremely difficult cases. In formulating general rules of procedure, you should operate from the usual. Not the norm (whatever that is), but at least the more usual. Then you must adjust those procedures as best you can, to account for the most difficult cases.

I feel very strongly about this because, by way of preparation for this conference, I read some of the proceedings of last year's meeting (2). Fairly early in the book a case was described, which I gather has been widely discussed and probably will again be discussed during this conference. In this case bone marrow was needed from a child to save the life of a sibling (*3, 4*). I do not know enough medicine to know what that procedure was and it does not say very much about it, so I interpret it as stated, that without the bone marrow the child would die, and the sibling was the only medically possible source of bone marrow. I also accept as fact the statement that there was minimal risk, which was described to me as approximately 1 chance in 40,000 of death. I did a good deal of troubled thinking about that particular case last night before I went to sleep, partly because the feelings I had about it, and still have, are contrary to my general principle, which is that research should not be done on people without their informed consent. I tried to think of what I would do if these two children, the sick one and the possible bone marrow donor, were my own children. After much tossing and turning, I decided that I would not ask for the consent of the sibling. I would say, "I will take you to the hospital so that we can get some bone marrow from you to save the life of your brother or sister." The reason that I would justify what seems to be a departure from a strongly held general principle, is not so much that this potential donor might not understand the risk of death, as that he certainly would not understand a quite different risk, that is, the risk of thinking the rest of his life that he had effectively murdered his brother or sister. My experience with children, and even teenage young people, is that they do not have a very strong sense of time. I can remember feeling, when I was in my first or second year at boarding school, that the seniors were much closer to the faculty than they were to me. I could not imagine being a senior. Seniors and faculty, grown-ups, lived in one world, while I, freshmen and sophomores, lived in another. This is an example of what I am saying about hard cases creating bad law, that it is possible to believe very strongly, and with almost no important reservations, in some kind of principle in conduct, and yet still be able to imagine a particular case in which you might feel you must act differently.

To return to the question of research and informed consent: The distinction that was made between research done on and research done for the patient seems to me extremely important, and very elegant. I looked for some way to phrase that kind of a distinction, but did not come up with anything nearly as nice. I would like to say, however, that drawing that line is not necessarily very easy. One cannot define a two-valued situation that makes it possible to say this is research on and this is research for. We are talking about a spectrum, not only of risk, but possibly of pain, discomfort, or simply fear. In fact, there are probably three spectra involving 1) what we are liable to gain, what the chances seem to be of this working out well; 2) the hazard, what we lose if it does not work out as we hope; and 3) what it costs the patient in the meanwhile. In other words, if two possible procedures had nearly equal chances of giving a favorable outcome, but one of these procedures involved great pain, anxiety, discomfort, or fright for a child, and the other was relatively painless and easy, they would not be equivalent. I think it would require a greater likelihood of a favorable outcome to justify a very painful or difficult procedure than it might one that is relatively easy. So we are dealing with spectra of outcome and risk and pain and discomfort. In the middle sections of these spectra there are going to be very difficult cases about which we might argue fiercely.

I take very strongly the general position that we have no right to do research involving people, regardless of risk, where their direct benefit is not involved or without their informed consent. Where informed consent cannot be given, as with very young children, and I mean *very* young, then I do not think we should do such research. That is, I do not think we have the right to use people who cannot give informed consent as research subjects in the hope of finding something that may be useful to somebody else.

Even if we set those general cases aside and talk about research for the benefit of a particular sick person, again the lines are not easily drawn. Obviously, we have no interest in trying out a procedure on a patient unless there is some reason for believing that in fact it will be better.

The next broad point is this: I believe that children are in fact capable of giving this kind of informed consent at very much younger ages than most people would suspect. I am not altogether sure where the line should be drawn. Perhaps I have to say something about informed consent. That is in itself not an easy notion. I believe informed consent implies a situation in which the people involved explain to the patient as honestly and fully as they can what is involved, what are the options, and what is the risk. What the patient makes of that information, none of us can know. We have no way of guessing the patient's ability to interpret correctly what is said, except insofar as he may ask other questions or indicate incomprehension by a dazed and bewildered expression. We have an obligation to make ourselves as clear as possible. However, generally speaking, I do not believe that we have the power or the right to make a lot of judgments about how capable the patient is of understanding what we are saying. In other words, there is a very, very heavy burden of proof on anyone who would say a particular patient is incapable of giving informed consent and therefore it is unnecessary to try to get it.

It seems to me that age is not a criterion per se. I know of 10-year-olds, even 8-year-olds, who seem as capable as many adults of understanding the options, choices, risks involved, and the different medical procedures, and of saying, "Well, I think we should do this or we should do that." This is not to say that all people would make those decisions equally well and wisely, or that children would always make them as wisely as older people. I do say that wisdom, even as regards these very difficult questions of life and death, is not a matter of age.

There is a notion among people who consider themselves believers in childhood or defenders of childhood that children are incapable of understanding death and should be shielded from talk about it or any knowledge of it. I do not believe this. I think history shows it is nonsense. Children lived with death, in the midst of death, until quite recently. They saw old people get sick and die. This is not the case anymore. I will be 54 years old in a few weeks and, except at my uncle's funeral (and not even then, actually; it was not an open casket), I have never seen a dead human body. And I do not think I am unusual among modern adults. I was in the submarines in the war where either everybody was killed or nobody was, so I did not see dead bodies in a situation in which a great many men do see them. I think it would be fair to say that, aside from during wartime and except for doctors, policemen, and some others, most people simply do not see death anymore. The limited knowledge we have of children facing their own deaths seems to me to support my very strong hunch that they are capable of facing it as bravely and wisely as older people. There has not been much written on this subject. John Gunther wrote a book about his son John, who died of a brain tumor, called *Death Be Not Proud* (5). More recently I read an account of an 8-year-old child who was dying of leukemia (6); these accounts support my feeling that children can and ought to be told about the possibility and risks of death.

Children are often said to have primitive perceptions of dying. They may consider dying equivalent to taking a journey. The objection is sometimes raised that giving children a choice in which death is the consequence of one of the options is unreasonable. However, a great many adults do not have a mature understanding of death, either. A great many adults think of death as a long journey, in fact, as a long journey to a much nicer place. I do not share that view. I rather envy those who have it, but one cannot have it by wishing; although, to be honest, I frankly do not feel greatly in need of it. I am, at the age of 54, still able to look with a certain amount of equanimity on the fact that it may be over. My dear friend A. S. Neill (the headmaster of the Summerhill School in England) said just a couple of months before he died, "I don't believe in the afterlife. I think it is like blowing out a candle. My only real regret is that I will not be able to find out what happened. I have a curiosity; I really have done everything on earth that I particularly wanted to do and I am too old and tired to have any more ambitions, but I am just curious about how it is going to turn out. I hate not seeing that. But otherwise, when I am gone, it's over." This is more or less my feeling. Although it may be painful and protracted, the outcome of leukemia treatment is nevertheless potentially very good. Therefore, a child can be given the choice between treatment and no treatment.

My belief is that a 6-year-old can understand about being able to get older, to go to school or drive a car, to do things that grown-ups do. We can paint a picture of life incorporating all the various things that the child has seen other people do. Kids want to grow up. Kids have no awareness of the innocence or marvelousness of childhood. They want to be big, to be able to do what other people can do. "Farewell, innocent happy childhood" would be their message. I think I could paint a realistic picture of those options: "On the one hand, we think you will be able to do all of those things. On the other hand you will not. You will not be able to go to grandmother's and do all those things you like to do, you are not going to be able to do them anymore." There are, of course, cases in which I would say no informed consent is possible. Then we give the treatment that we are pretty sure will make the child well. My belief is that that age is much younger than we have thought.

Ease with death is not necessarily the result of experience with life. I do not think that my father, who died at 85, had an informed, realistic, or mature approach to death. I was very acutely aware of this when he died. It was about the same time that I had spent $3\frac{1}{2}$ hours in the company of A. S. Neill. He was almost gone, he died just a few months later. He knew he was going to die, and had reached a point where he could hardly eat anymore, so this was our last meeting. We spent a long time talking, much of the time about death, and what it felt like to be near death and know that you are going to die within a few weeks or days. How he looked back on life, that was the topic.

Very late in his life I came to know the composer Frank Martin, who then lived in Holland but was born in Switzerland. I saw him a couple of times, again very nearly before he died, in his mid-80's; a lovely old man. Again we talked about what it was like to get up each morning not really knowing whether this might be your last day of life, and how he dealt with it, and how he composed in the face of it. I was never able to have any such conversations with my father, and nobody else did. Indeed, this very expensive, elaborately run, very kindly institution where he spent his old days had made death a taboo. I do not know if the word had been spoken there in the previous 5 years. So I do not think experience has necessarily anything to do with maturity of insight about death.

Wanting death, asking to stop treatment, is a difficult topic in medicine. I watched both my parents in their final days, not in the sense of being there every day, but I paid them regular visits. They both died in that very stylish establishment that was called, ironically, a convalescent home. It was a convalescent home where nobody convalesced. You left feet first and everyone knew it, but that was a forbidden topic of conversation in that place. Their doctor was a very nice man and I liked him. He was humane. He used to say constantly to me, "We are not going to go through any medical heroics." In other words, we were not going to have them all wired up with pipes and tubes and so forth, we just wanted to make them comfortable. Yet from my visits it was obvious to me that some months before they died, both were ready to stop. They had had enough.

I can remember my mother lying in bed. She reached a point where she had to be fed with a syringe. I remember one scene in particular. Her nurse was a very nice woman whom my parents had liked very much. My mother was past the point of liking and not liking, but had been good friends with the nurse, so this is not a story against that certain nurse. She was feeding her with a syringe and my mother was simply holding the food. She did not want to eat anymore, did not want to swallow. The nurse was saying, "Now, Mrs. Holt." There is a ghastly way people talk to very old people, turning the time clock backwards, as though they were babies again. The nurse said, "Oh, I can see you are holding that food in your mouth. Now you swallow that food, you know," etc. My mother was always a stubborn woman. She did not want to do it, and after a while faint hints were made, such as "We don't want to have to feed you through tubes."

My father had Parkinson's disease, which made him unable to swallow without getting food down his windpipe. So he was constantly told to keep his fluids up. This was to keep him "comfortable." He had to eat. I could almost hear him think, "Why do I have to eat? What am I eating for?" Intake of fluids was constantly pushed, and all this was carefully metered. His urine was measured and he was lavished with nursing attention. Every time he took a sip of water, some went down his windpipe, which was of course followed by a coughing spasm. Every meal he ate was agonizing. I remember him talking in a kind of exhausted way after some food had gotten down his windpipe and he coughed for about half a minute trying to get it up. He said, "Sometimes I don't see what the point of all this is."

So the question of when to say, "No more, that is enough," is as difficult for adults as it is for children. Certainly, opinion about this is changing rapidly in medicine. It is becoming a very live issue. Yet I think I am more ready to give most people the right to say, "That is enough, no more, just let me go," than the majority of my fellow citizens or probably than the majority of doctors and medical people. I think I would be more ready than most people to extend this right to even quite a young child. I feel that what is humane and proper for adults is humane and proper for children. If we are talking about children who are beneath the age of consent, we have to make that decision ourselves. If we reach the point where we really do not believe any longer that we are going to be able to keep this child alive, how can we inflict more pain?

It is not necessary to separate guidelines for children from those for adults. In the areas of discipline, which may seem at first to be very different from the areas of medicine, relevant analogies can nevertheless be found. One of the things I say to people all over the country about children, even very, very young children, is that they are interested in our rules and want to know what they are. Most of the time, except when temporarily swept away by passion, children want to obey them. They are acutely social animals. What they are quick to perceive and tend very strongly to dislike and, in various ways and degrees, to resist are rules that quite obviously are set up especially for them and have nothing to do with the rules by which adults live. They become aware of that discrepancy quite quickly and they do not like it. In general, they want to do as we do. This means that in almost any situation, including a medical situation, they are interested in how people behave, what big people do; that is pretty much the way they want to behave. Therefore, I think it is perfectly reasonable to apply our conceptions of what are proper, healthful, helpful relationships between doctors and adult patients to children. However, to try to make children play a role in the classroom or the sickroom that we would never dream of asking of an adult or of ourselves seems to me to be a mistake.

There is, of course, a special problem when the wishes and demands of the parents counter those of the child. Then we have a legal problem. In general, the law does not acknowledge that children have the right to informed consent about anything. I think it is a mistake, a very serious wrong; but it is not likely to change in the near future. Practically speaking, I guess it is not going to be possible for doctors to give a child informed consent if the parents do not want the child to have it. I do not think doctors or medical people have the right to say to parents, "No, we are not interested in what you think, we are going to ask the child." I guess you would be subject to lawsuits and all kinds of criticism. Ethically speaking, ideally, I certainly think the parents ought to have their day in court; I think if the parents want their child to do something, they have every right to put their case to the child as strongly as possible, because they have an interest, too. But if possible, I would give the final choice to the child. However, for legal reasons you cannot always, so the parents' words may be the only prevailing ones.

Not all children are ready to make choices, and parents have had some hand in creating that ability to be wise. A child who can act independently is precisely the kind of child whom the parents are likely to allow to make any important medical decisions anyway. If we imagine the by no means hypothetical child whose parents have never allowed to make any choices and who is now in the hospital, I do not believe those same parents are going to let that child make choices about treatment. So there is less conflict between the parents' restrictions and the right to choose than might appear. A very dependent child might very well say when given a choice, even if the parents did not intervene, "I don't know. Ask Mommy, ask Daddy." The child who has had no experience at making choices, might not want to make them.

In general, then, as I have been saying all along, children are very much more intelligent than we give them credit for being. They are much more like us than unlike us. The differences between young people and old people are no greater than the differences between two people of the same age with respect to things like courage or cowardice or stoicism or the willingness to face unpleasant reality and so on. There are important differences between human beings with respect to almost anything, but they do not seem to me to correlate in any important way with age. If I were to try to condense a great deal of what I have been saying and thinking into a short statement, which obviously should be qualified and does not apply to all extreme cases, it would be that, by and large, sound humane medical practice for children is the same as sound humane medical practice for adults.

One must always remain aware of what informed consent means. To inform means to represent the options and the possibilities; consent means "yes." My point earlier was that we cannot make judgments, we simply have no way of making judgments, about the quality of the processes that go on in the patient's mind. We can inform and we can give the patient the right to consent. Many feel that the questions raised in informed consent for research are too difficult for the child. Obviously, there is no point in using a technical vocabulary that is meaningless to the patient. But in every case I think it is possible to talk about risks or pain or whatever it may be in language that ordinary people, including young children, can understand. We do not know what is going on in the mind of any patient, no matter what his age; we get clues if the patient asks questions, which we then try to answer as honestly as we can. But that is all we can do, to do the best we can to make ourselves understood and hope that we have been understood. In this, as in all human communications, there is a huge element of uncertainty and risk, and I do not think we can avoid it. Obviously, a child who has not yet acquired language is going to be pretty hard to talk to about treatments. I do not know about 3- and 4-year-old children, but children reach the stage quite early at which they are, in fact, capable of thinking sensibly, morally, and responsibly.

Do we indeed ask for informed consent? Do children of any age get to participate in the decisions? Does it in fact happen that a 12-year-old can refuse treatment? Does it in fact happen? Is a 12-year-old, in fact, given that option? Can a 13- or a 14-year-old say "No, I won't let you treat me!"? My hunch is that it happens rather rarely, because asking for informed consent is asking the child's approval.

You have to be careful that you understand that. Informed consent is asking the child's approval. That demands no prior discussion to coerce the child to agree with you. I do not believe in such discussions; I think they are wrong. They happen all the time. In fact, I think such discussions can be terribly phony. One of the things I say to teachers of young children, nursery schools, day care centers, parents, is "Do not say, 'Okay'; do not say, 'It is time for our nap, okay?' or, 'Now let's take off our coats, okay?'" It seems to me extremely important to decide in what matters you are going to give the child a choice, in which case you give a choice, or in what situations you are not, in which case you do not pretend to.

You have to decide that before you start. That was why I spent an hour or more twisting and turning, thinking about the bone marrow. To give somebody a choice means risking that they may not choose the way you choose, and you are stuck with it. As I keep saying to parents, "Look, if you are determined that your child shall stop playing with that toy, get dressed, get in the car, and go with you somewhere, then you say, courteously, as people speak to adults, 'We have to go now, so would you please put that away' and, you know, hat and coat and here we go. Even give a little physical assistance if it seems necessary, but again in a spirit of courtesy; regret that you are interrupting an important activity, which is how people talk to me when they have to interrupt something I am doing. If in fact you do not care which way it turns out, then you offer the choice."

I suggested that my basis for not giving the child a choice in the bone marrow situation was his inability to understand the impact of perhaps feeling in later life that he had murdered his sibling if he refused to donate. The question then arises, to what degree can children understand more abstract needs, like the good of mankind. Should I make the choice for them also in such value judgments? Suppose the bone marrow is for someone else, or that you do not know for whom it might be. This to me presents a medical difficulty. I am ignorant. I assume that the reason that the sibling's bone marrow was necessary was because of some problem of incompatibility or genetics; so the statement "If you do not give that bone marrow nobody else can, and therefore the sibling will die" represents the actual facts. If we are now talking about giving bone marrow for someone in general, I am medically at sea, I do not know. However, we could speak about blood transfusion, about the questions of blood donors. I do not think we should take blood from people without their consent. It is possible that there are exceptions. A friend of mine has a very rare blood type, understands very well its scarcity, and therefore feels a heavier personal duty to contribute blood to the blood bank than some of us might, in fact, than I do. I do not give blood really as often as I ought; I am busy, lazy. I do not mind the procedure, but I always seem to have something else to do when I ought to do it and I make no particular defense of myself. I think I might feel wrong or differently if I had a very rare kind of blood. I think this is something that a child with a very rare and valuable kind of blood also might understand. It would be perfectly possible to talk to a child who was dying about the possibility of giving his or her corneas or perhaps other organs to save other people's lives. This is something I would not hesitate to bring up. I would ask it in the same spirit with which I would ask an adult, "Will you give your corneas after you are dead?" Some people are perfectly willing to do that but others have strong, different feelings about their corpses, and they will not. However, in any case, that is the choice I would give.

The decision whether or not a child is ready to give informed consent is difficult. Whether a child is emotionally mature enough I cannot presume to judge. I cannot presume to know that about anybody in the whole world. It is not a matter of intellect or knowledge. I am not talking about intrinsic ability. I am not talking about IQ or anything comparable to that. I am talking about something quite different. I am talking about something called wisdom. I am not a Catholic or, in any sense of the word that I would understand, even religious. But the Catholic Church has traditionally held that moral responsibility begins at the age of 7. From the age of 7 you are responsible. I think this represents an accurate historical understanding of what human beings are like. Even though it may not be an absolute measure in all cases, we should be prepared to accept that moral responsibility of the child in medical situations as well.

REFERENCES

1. Axline, V. M. 1976. Dibbs: In Search of Self. Ballantine Books Inc., New York.
2. van Eys, J. (ed.). 1977. The Truly Cured Child. University Park Press, Baltimore.
3. Richie, E. 1977. Biomedical research: for the patient or on the patient? In: J. van Eys (ed.), The Truly Cured Child, pp. 27–37. University Park Press, Baltimore.
4. Levine, M. D., Camitta, B. M., Nathan, D., and Curran, W. J. 1975. The medical ethics of bone marrow transplantation in childhood. J. Pediatr. 86: 145.
5. Gunther, J. 1953. Death Be Not Proud. Harper and Row, New York.
6. Moustakas, C. 1972. The dying self within the living self. In: C. Moustakas (ed.), The Child's Discovery of Himself, pp. 8–27. Ballantine Books, Inc., New York.

THE MEDICAL IMPERATIVE

THE MEDICAL DIMENSIONS OF RESEARCH ON CHILDREN
An Introduction

H. Grant Taylor

The use of chemicals to control malignant disease has grown in the last 25 years from little more than a concept to an accepted mode of therapy. The success of the endeavor has depended upon several related programs, such as basic animal research, drug screening programs, and extended, carefully supervised clinical trials. However, if it were not for the willingness of parents and patients to join with their medical staffs in making possible these studies, the program of pooling patient data from a variety of sources, collected to meet the demands of a previously agreed upon protocol, would have failed.

The National Cancer Chemotherapy Program of the Division of Cancer Treatment of the National Cancer Institute is directed toward locating effective anticancer chemicals and shepherding these agents through clinical trials. Foremost among its components is the drug screening program, which tests a large number of chemical substances each year. It is the largest screening program of its kind in the world. Related to the screening program is the independent or ancillary studies component, which is also a very extensive effort. The last component is the cooperative clinical research program, which involves scientific representatives from over 220 institutions who meet in study groups to prepare protocols and report on patients previously committed to study. Basic to the success of the entire program, of course, is the willingness of patients and parents to participate in the protocols.

In the early days of the program, cooperative groups were formed. There was no way to study rare tumors other than by pooling the data of the available patients under study. Some of the tumors are so rare that the experience acquired, irrespective of the care taken to document the disease, would have been meaningless.

The benefits derived from pooling patient data initially, however, were diminished by the fact that many of the patients committed to study programs had already received therapy and in most instances were terminal. In spite of many failures, difficulties arising from toxicity, untimely death, and adverse feelings, the basic principles for an ultimately successful program in cancer chemotherapy were established. Although some were bitterly disappointed, most parents were willing to balance the optimal patient care and modest prolongation of life against the drug toxicity and failures in disease control. Parents could justifiably question the prolongation of suffering, but most had confidence that the pain would be controlled. Many understood that the participation of their children in a study was a way of helping someone else's child. Every parent of a child with cancer admitted to a cancer treatment center today owes a great debt to those children and parents.

Giving consent today for a child to participate in a study protocol is not so difficult as in the past. The odds now greatly favor a more successful outcome. Better data are available on which to base a decision, but those data were only made possible by the cooperation of parents and children who participated earlier.

THERAPEUTIC RESEARCH AS A NECESSARY MODE OF MANAGEMENT

Wataru W. Sutow

If the purpose of this workshop is to establish some guidelines for the future, it is reasonable to review what has happened in the past. Accordingly, data regarding two childhood cancers, Wilms' tumor and osteosarcoma, are presented. The data are examined to derive perspectives on where and how some of the issues discussed at this workshop might have arisen.

These comments are limited to childhood cancer. In children, cancer remains the leading medical cause of death. Next to accidents, it kills more children under 15 years of age than any other cause. It can also be stated with near certainty that, without effective treatment, children with cancer will die from cancer. Thus, in the management of children with cancer, every therapy decision has a direct bearing on the life or death of the patient. As the result of persistent and increasingly effective chemotherapy, the prognosis for several childhood cancers, including Wilms' tumor and osteosarcoma, has improved significantly in recent years (Figure 1).

Wilms' tumor is a cancer of the kidney that occurs most frequently in children under 4 years of age (*1*). Without treatment, all children with Wilms' tumor will die from progression of the tumor. With intensive multimodal treatment today, under favorable clinical circumstances, more than 90% of the patients survive (*2*).

Certain key events can be recognized that have brought about the control of this cancer. The first was the acceptance of the fact that surgical removal of the cancer is necessary. During this period, which spanned the early decades of this century, important improvements in surgical techniques also occurred. Developments in anesthesiology and in operative and postoperative support of patients virtually eliminated

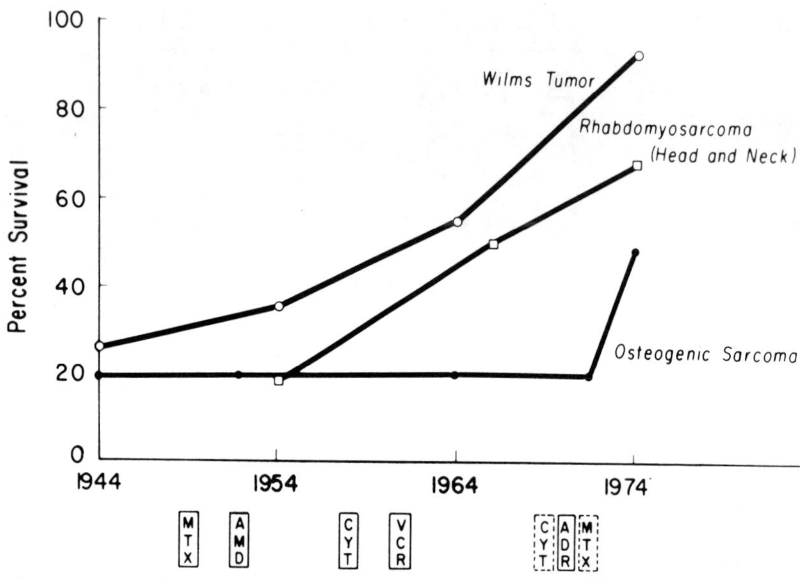

Figure 1. Improving prognosis in childhood cancer, Percentage of survival is correlated chronologically with the introduction of effective chemotherapeutic agents. *MTX*
= methotrexate, *AMD* = actinomycin D, *CYT* = cyclophosphamide, *VCR* = vincristine, *ADR* = adriamycin. CYT within *broken line* indicates development of large dose
intermittent schedule for cyclophosphamide. *MTX* within *broken line* indicates the use
of massive doses of methotrexate in conjunction with citrovorum factor rescue. From
Sutow, W. W. 1975. Chemotherapy in the management of childhood solid tumors. In:
Cancer Chemotherapy—Fundamental Concepts and Recent Advances. Year Book
Medical Publishers, Inc., Chicago. p. 205.

operative complications as a cause of death. However, the cure rate
from surgery alone plateaued at about 15% to 20% (*1*). This meant
that 80% or more of children with Wilms' tumor were still dying.

The application of radiation therapy in patients with Wilms'
tumor began another phase. As knowledge expanded and techniques
were refined, this modality also added significantly to the control of
Wilms' tumor. The combination of radiation therapy and surgery was
a natural step. By 1945, the overall control rate of Wilms' tumor had
improved to about 40% of all patients, but once again the survival
curve leveled.

The discovery, evaluation, and utilization of drugs mark the current phase, covering the past 20 years. By 1967 it was clear that
actinomycin D had improved the survival rate in children with Wilms'
tumor. It was also clear that vincristine was effective. Which drug was

better and how effective a combination would be was unestablished. In 1969 a national study was begun to answer these questions. One other important question was also tackled: if the tumor were completely removed surgically, could postoperative radiotherapy to the tumor bed be safely omitted if chemotherapy were given?

After 6 years and over 600 patients, the answers are just now emerging (2). Vincristine, the newer drug, was as effective as actinomycin D, the so-called standard therapy, but their combination in an investigative regimen was significantly more effective than either drug alone. If precise staging of the extent of the disease was carried out, it was also possible to omit postoperative radiation therapy in certain clinical situations.

In the management of Wilms' tumor, therefore, as the control rate has improved progressively from 0% to above 90%, it has become evident that investigative therapy has to be considered, used, and evaluated at each of several points: surgery, innovations in supportive care, radiation therapy, and chemotherapy. At each point, the results of certain investigative approaches have proved better than the results of the standard therapy. Or, put another way, the best current standard therapy was at one time a new investigative therapy.

Even as we stand today at the very forefront of cancer therapy with the control of Wilms' tumor, we are already recognizing new problems. We are beginning to realize that a near 100% cure rate is not enough. Some of the patients who were cured of cancer are dying, not of recurrent cancer, but of causes related to the treatment itself. In one study, 9 of 140 patients with Wilms' tumor who were disease-free at 3 years died later of therapy-related complications. (3). So we face new challenges: how to refine our therapeutic approaches and reduce the risks of late effects.

Osteosarcoma is cancer of the bone occurring in children, adolescents, and young adults. It is a highly malignant cancer in which we have just recently begun to improve our cure rates. Like Wilms' tumor, it is uniformly and rapidly fatal if no treatment is given.

With surgery alone, the survival rate ranged between 5% and 15% (4). Even with amputation, over a period of decades 80% to 95% of the patients died. The addition of radiation to the treatment program did not improve the survival rate; but now, as the result of investigative chemotherapy studies, we believe that at least 55% will be cured (5). The cure rate may be even higher with increasingly intensive therapy programs.

The progressive development of adjunctive chemotherapy for osteosarcoma illustrates the time-consuming and often frustrating efforts that are required to bring any cancer under even partial control. Around 1962 it was demonstrated that osteosarcoma may, in selected instances, be sensitive to a drug such as phenylalanine mustard (PAM). However, 14 patients treated with PAM as adjuvant chemotherapy fared no better than others. In about 1966 we were having considerable success with a three-drug combination of vincristine, actinomycin D, and cyclophosphamide against another cancer of childhood, rhabdomyosarcoma. This combination was modified and utilized in the primary treatment of osteosarcoma. Of 12 patients treated, four remained disease-free. This cure rate of 33% was better than any result reported up to that time.

In about 1970 a new drug, adriamycin, showed significant antitumor effect in osteosarcoma. A short time later the administration of methotrexate in massive doses in conjunction with citrovorum factor rescue regimen also produced responses in patients with metastatic osteosarcoma. As a result, several chemotherapy programs utilizing the drugs singly and in various combinations are now being evaluated at major cancer centers.

The current status of control of osteosarcoma is indicated by survival curves derived from a retrospective analysis of the data from patients treated at M. D. Anderson Hospital. Figure 2 compares the survival rates of those who received investigative chemotherapy and those who did not (6). The difference in survival rates is highly significant. Seventy-nine percent of the patients who had amputation plus the current type of chemotherapy were living after 2 years. In comparison, 66% of the patients who did not receive the current type of chemotherapy were dead after 2 years.

The options in the treatment of osteosarcoma today are several:

1. Refuse amputation and accept the almost sure failure of disease control.
2. Accept surgery, but refuse all adjunctive chemotherapy for a 1 in 5 chance of disease-free survival.
3. Accept surgery plus one of several adjunctive chemotherapy programs used in the past 4 or 5 years for an even chance of survival at some cost in toxicity.
4. Accept surgery plus an investigative program for a possible better chance of survival, but also some added risk of potential drug toxicity.

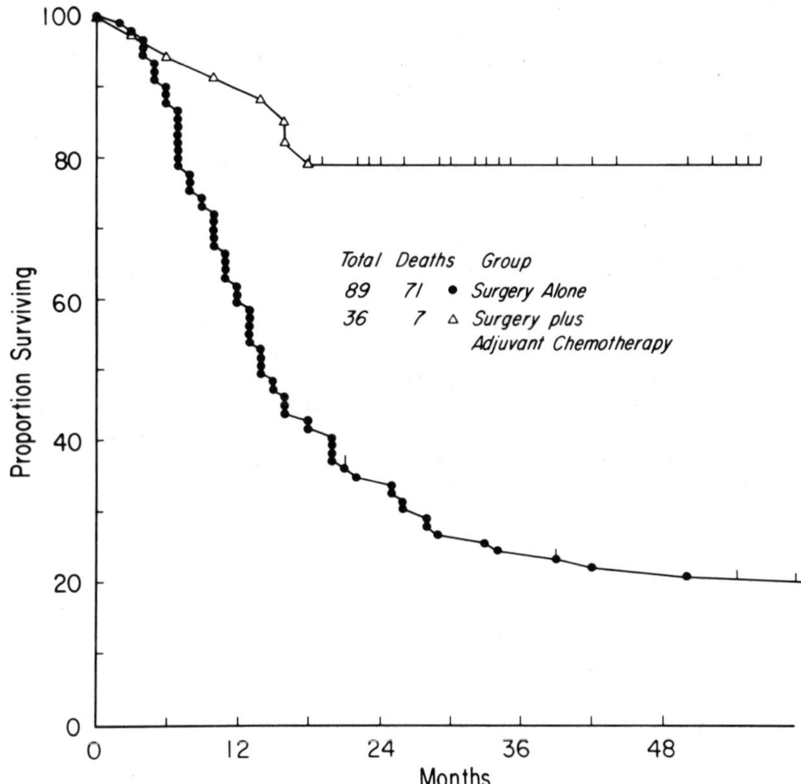

Figure 2.   Survival curves for those receiving amputation plus chemotherapy and for those undergoing amputation alone. From Gehan, E. A., Sutow, W. W., Uribe-Botero, G., Romsdahl, M., and Smith, T. L. Osteosarcoma: the M. D. Anderson experience, 1950–1974. In: Immunotherapy of Cancer: Present Status of Trials in Man. Terry, William D. and Windohorst, Dorothy, Editors. © 1977, Raven Press, New York.

If the outcome of a treatment is accurately predictable, there is no need for any investigation of that treatment. If the outcome is not predictable, however, all such treatment (regardless of its general acceptance or usage) is categorically investigative in principle.

Until the cure rate approaches 100% under all clinical circumstances, with therapy that has acceptable toxicity and minimum risk of late effects, we need to continually improve our therapeutic capabilities. As long as that need exists, an investigative posture must be maintained to attain our goals with the greatest degree of certainty in the shortest possible time.

REFERENCES

1. Sutow, W. W. 1975. Wilms' tumor. Methods Cancer Res. 13:31–65.
2. D'Angio, G. J., Evans, A. E., Breslow, N., Beckwith, B., Bishop, H., Feigl, P., Goodwin, W., Leape, L. L., Sinks, L. F., Sutow, W. W., Tefft, M., and Wolff, J. 1976. The treatment of Wilms' tumor: Results of the National Wilms' Tumor Study. Cancer 38:633–646.
3. Li, F. P., Bishop, Y., and Katsioules, C. 1975. Survival in Wilms' tumour. Lancet 1:41–42.
4. Friedman, M. A., and Carter, S. K. 1972. The therapy of osteogenic sarcoma: current status and thoughts for the future. J. Surg. Oncol. 4:482–510.
5. Sutow, W. W., Gehan, E. A., Vietti, T. J., Frias, A. E., and Dyment, P. G. 1976. Multidrug chemotherapy in primary treatment of osteosarcoma. J. Bone and Joint Surg. 58(A):629–633.
6. Gehan, E. A., Sutow, W. W., Uribe-Botero, G., Romsdahl, M., and Smith, T. L. 1977. Osteosarcoma: the M. D. Anderson experience, 1950–1974. In: Immunotherapy of Cancer: Present Status of Trials in Man. Raven Press, New York.

CHILDREN AS THERAPEUTIC ORPHANS

Margaret P. Sullivan

Several years ago I was asked to participate in a student-organized course at Rice University by speaking on the topic "What Is a Pediatrician?" Reflections as well as research led me to conclude at that time that pediatricians are much like internists with one additional attribute, a liking for children. In their specialty training, pediatricians learn the intricacies of growth and development that are reflected in physical, metabolic, and endocrine changes; they learn the infectious processes peculiar to an immune system that is being educated through exposure, and they learn the early detection of the myriad genetically transmitted disorders. In short, they learn that the child is not a "little adult." Differences in fluid and electrolyte requirements between younger children and adults are recognized by all. Important pharmacologic differences are found between children and adults in the absorption, distribution, metabolism, and excretion of many agents, including aspirin, diphenylhydantoin, primidone, and diazepam (*1*), penicillin (*2*), and chloramphenicol (*3*). Fortunately, metabolic and pharmacologic differences between the child and the adult lessen as the child grows older, disappearing, for all practical purposes, after the age of 12.

In the educational process, the pediatrician becomes not only the child's physician, but also the child's advocate, speaking for those who cannot as yet speak for themselves. This advocacy often extends beyond medicine into social, ethical, and educational aspects of the child's life.

In the role of the advocate, Dr. Harry Shirkey, in editorials in the *Journal of Pediatrics* and the *Southern Medical Journal,* called the attention of the medical community to an insidious practice that was making children into what he termed "therapeutic orphans" (*4, 5*). As used by Dr. Shirkey, the term implies that children are being deprived not of their parents, but of therapy that is as much their due as it is adults'. This deprival results from the lack of pharmacokinetic data and dosage recommendations for children in the package insert. As background for understanding, it should be remembered that the thalidomide disaster resulted in regulations requiring drug manufacturers to provide evidence of the safety and the efficacy of their product when making a new drug application before marketing. Information supporting the claims of safety and efficacy, approved indications for use, dosage recommendations, and toxicity data must appear on the package insert distributed with the drug. In subsequent advertising and promotional claims, the manufacturer is bound by the contents of the package inserts. Although the recommendations in the package insert are not considered legally binding to the physician, they are a strong deterrent to use in any other manner. In short, physicians fear malpractice suits should they not act strictly in accord with the package insert.

Paradoxically, regulations designed to insure drug safety and effectiveness, particularly in children, have resulted more and more frequently in such disclaimers as: "Not recommended for use in infants and children," "Not recommended for children less than 12 years of age," "Clinical studies have been insufficient to establish any recommendation for use in infants and children," and "Should not be given to children."

Disclaimers and the failure to make dosage recommendations for children may be attributed to various factors, including:

1. The potentially small children's market for drugs compared to that for adults. Pediatricians are not ungrateful for "service items" many pharmaceutical houses make available. They also recognize that sound business practices require financial return on money and time invested in drug development. Drug houses are in business to make money. Cancer drugs in particular have a small market and thus yield a poor return to the developer.
2. The unavailability of suitable children for study except in large pediatric centers. Ethical considerations demand that new drugs be tested in the populations of intended use, as determined by both age and diagnosis. Pharmacologic studies would, therefore, require interinstitutional collaboration with manufacturers to shorten the time required to bring the drug to market.
3. Technical difficulties of maintaining IV's, completing urine collections, and obtaining serum specimens from children.

4. A shortage of qualified pediatric clinical investigators. Training programs for pediatric pharmacologists exist at only 10 centers.
5. Ethical considerations concerning the child as a research subject, including individual vs. class or group benefits and ability of the child or the parent to give informed consent for research investigations.

The extent of therapeutic orphaning was assessed in 1973 by Dr. John Wilson, a pediatric pharmacologist at Vanderbilt Hospital, using computer analysis of data contained in the *Physicians' Desk Reference* (PDR) (*6*). The PDR is a compilation of package insert information on marketed drugs that is published annually by Medical Economics Company. It is circulated to well over half a million physicians, paramedical personnel, and hospitals. A survey by the FDA showed 89% of physicians considered the PDR their most useful source of information (*7*). The Wilson study showed the PDR to be the most frequently used source of drug information at Vanderbilt Hospital; 50% of the house staff used this reference more frequently than any other. The analysis was limited to medications given systemically. Disclaimers for pediatric use were categorized as "contraindication," "use with caution," and "use restricted by age."

As shown in Table 1, a disclaimer for use in children was found in about 16% of trade name medicines; the percentage of disclaimers for single ingredient preparations was higher than that for fixed drug combinations. Further study of age-related disclaimers showed restriction for age <12 to be most frequent, occuring in 33% of all medicines; restriction for age <6 was less common (20%) and for age <1 month

Table 1.   Summary of recommendations for use of drugs on children in PDR (1973)

Category	Restricted use in children (%)		
	All medicines ($N = 2000$)	Single agents ($N = 1015$)	Combination medicines ($N = 985$)
Not to be used on children	3	3	2
Caution in use on children	3	5	1
Age restrictions given	10	12	9
Sum	16	20	12

From Wilson, J. T. Basic Therapeutic Aspects of Perinatal Pharmacology (Monograph of the Mario Negri Institute for Pharmacological Research), Morselli, Paolo L., Garattini, Silvio and Sereni, Fabio, Editors. © 1975, Raven Press, New York.

Table 2.   Summary of information on dosage for children in PDR (1973)

| | Lack of dose information in children (%) | | |
| | --- | --- | --- |
Category	All medicines ($N = 2000$)	Single agents ($N = 1015$)	Combination medicines ($N = 985$)
No dose for children given	50	41	58
Age restricted information	12	7	17
Sum	62	48	75

From Wilson, J. T. Basic Therapeutic Aspects of Perinatal Pharmacology (Monograph of the Mario Negri Institute for Pharmacological Research), Morselli, Paolo L., Garattini, Silvio and Sereni, Fabio, Editors. © 1975, Raven Press, New York.

very infrequent (13%). Use in children was further limited in 62% of PDR entries by the absence of dose information for children (Table 2). Lack of dose information was most frequent for age <6. The percentage of age-related disclaimers was similar for single ingredient medications and fixed combinations. The same pattern was found when medications were analyzed by generic name.

In most instances, the original package insert continues to be used without modification, even when it has become inadequate and obsolete. No mechanism exists to force the removal of disclaimers or to require the addition of dose information for children.

In a mini-survey of my 1974 PDR for information on the eight most frequently used cancer drugs for children, two agents were found to have been omitted; dactinomycin was listed by name only and adriamycin was not included. Vincristine, Cytoxan, and methotrexate did not specify doses for children. Prednisone, Purinethol, and Cytosar had general statements as to doses in children.

Therapeutic orphaning is now being addressed by both the FDA and the Committee on Drugs of the American Academy of Pediatrics, for children must have rational drug therapy made available to them. Drugs available to adults can no longer be withheld from children or given to them under less than optimum circumstances. Pediatric pharmacology must be expanded to provide the studies necessary to generate pediatric dosage information for every new drug marketed that has a potential use in children.

REFERENCES

1.   Wilson, J. T. 1976. Special problems for drugs used in children. South. Med. J. 69:779–786.

2. Barnett, H. L., McNamara, H., Schultz, S., and Tompsett, R. 1949. Renal clearances of sodium penicillin G, procaine penicillin G, and insulin in infants and children. Pediatrics 3:418–422.
3. Burns, L. E., Hodgeman, J. E., and Cass, A. B. 1959. Fatal circulatory collapse in premature infants receiving chloramphenicol. N. Engl. J. Med. 261:1318–1321.
4. Shirkey, H. 1968. Therapeutic orphans. J. Pediatr. 72:119–120.
5. Shirkey, H. 1970. Therapeutic orphans: who speaks for children? South. Med. J. 63:1361–1363.
6. Wilson, J. T. 1975. Pragmatic assessment of medicines available for young children and pregnant or breast-feeding women. In: P. L. Morselli, S. Garattini, and F. Sereni (eds.), Basic and Therapeutic Aspects of Perinatal Pharmacology. Raven Press, New York.
7. Ruskin, A., Knopp, D. S., and Nierllette, H. P. (eds.). 1974. Survey of Drug Information Needs and Communication Problem of Practicing Physicians. National Technical Information Service, Springfield, Va.

THE IMPORTANCE OF RESEARCH ON CHILDREN
A Geneticist's View

Rodney R. Howell

Several issues must enter into consideration of research on children. With some of these, I would like to apply what I feel represent some common sense attitudes. We must consider what are the reasonable risks of any proposed study and what are the risks of acquiring such data. If it is important to have new data on children or to develop new treatments, what are the consequences of not having such information or such therapy, and what are the alternatives? My perspective is primarily that of a geneticist; issues of therapeutic trials have been reviewed clearly by Dr. Sutow in these proceedings.

One of the first areas that I would like to consider is the apparently simple problem of normal data in childhood. There are ample data to indicate that one cannot extrapolate from adult values. This is true for virtually any parameter, such as hemoglobin, blood electrolytes, blood glucose, or other simple compounds in the blood. A large amount of data, both in humans and in animals, demonstrates conclusively that dynamic changes occur in virtually all such parameters during childhood. Therefore, it is essential, if we are to study and interpret data in a sick child or a child with any congenital or acquired disorder, that we know exactly the value of the compound being examined in the normal child.

The question that then presents itself is, what is a source of these normal data and how are they to be acquired? It has been said that one good way to acquire "normal data" is to use excess serum or other blood samples left in the clinical laboratory from routine studies in children who are hospitalized for a variety of conditions. This is not a scientifically acceptable method of obtaining normal values for patently obvious reasons. First, normal children are not hospitalized.

Additionally, blood is rarely obtained from children felt to be completely normal except for very small quantities, such as for hematocrits. Therefore, data obtained in this fashion are questionable.

The only option that remains is to identify normal children and obtain material from them. Children from whom normal values are obtained should, at the point the studies are done, be indeed normal, such as those seen for health maintenance and not for illness. Such children are often unable to comprehend the nature of the test, let alone provide informed consent. Therefore, the only source of informed consent in these instances is the parents. Many questions have been raised about the validity of parental consent in such studies, but the need is obvious.

The next question is, what is one justified in doing in the completely normal child? That is open to wide interpretation, but I feel that one is justified in taking simple measurements of such things as blood constituents, height, and weight; things that do not significantly infringe on the patient. Obviously, what is considered significant is also open to interpretation. Let me illustrate with some recent studies what we have done in establishing the absolute normal values of amino acids in the serum of infants and children.

Many conditions of childhood are associated with variations in serum and urinary amino acids. However, most available normal data were obtained some years ago, and since that time there has been a virtual revolution in methodology. Therefore, no excellent normal values were available for our current use. Before embarking on these studies, we modified our amino acid equipment so we could assess the concentrations of these materials in the smallest possible blood sample. Nearly a year's work and great expense were needed to modify the equipment so that these components could be assessed in 50 microliters of blood (which necessitates drawing only a few drops of blood from a finger. We then approached a group of parents whose children were being followed in our facilities for health maintenance. At the time these children were assessed as healthy by their physicians, parental consent was requested and received, in virtually all instances, to obtain small blood samples from the finger. The parents were told that this was to establish normal blood values and that their children, as far as could be perceived, were completely normal. It is possible, in this size study (more than 100 normal children), that we might have established that certain patients were abnormal. We certainly would have attempted to notify the parents of this abnormality or variation, particularly if anything could be accomplished therapeutically.

Some other kinds of information from children would be very valuable, but because of risk, discomfort, and other considerations, do not seem justified. For instance, it might be useful to know the exact value for pulmonary artery pressure in a group of normal children so that they might be compared to children with congenital heart disease. However, to do cardiac catheterization in normal children would clearly not be indicated. Therefore, such information would have to be inferred from the study of children who require catheterization for therapeutic reasons. We must accept that certain values are less than optimal. What sorts of risks, pain, discomfort, etc., are acceptable for the normal child is open to varying opinions, so there is a need for a diverse human experimentation committee, such as operates in all institutions where medical research is proceeding.

One area that needs comment relates to screening programs. The most widely publicized screening program during childhood, at the current time, is that done for phenylketonuria, a rare condition in which a genetically determined deficiency of the enzyme phenylalanine hydroxylase results in inability to utilize the amino acid phenylalanine. The important consequence of this disorder is profound mental retardation. The average untreated victim of phenylketonuria has an intelligence quotient below 20 and is characteristically hyperactive. The combination of hyperactivity and profound mental retardation means that most of these unfortunate children who have a normal life expectancy, spend a lifetime in an institution for the retarded.

In most states, all infants have a blood test for abnormalities of phenylalanine that would suggest the presence of phenylketonuria. Opponents of the program consider this a substantial invasion of the rights of the child, and have questioned its validity. I think that such arguments are ill-conceived and can only be seriously supported by the uninformed. Phenylketonuria cannot be diagnosed and substantiated without blood tests. In order to be efficacious, treatment must begin before any other symptoms appear. Therefore, the patient must be tested before the onset of symptoms. Because this disease is inherited in an autosomal recessive fashion, it may appear in families in which no family history of it exists; therefore, prospective screening (except in the rare family in which the disease is known to exist) is essential.

I know of no informed parent who could provide a reasonable objection to having this test done in the newborn period. Therefore, it seems highly appropriate to me that this test be done routinely on all children and that parental permission not be required. The screening program for and treatment of phenylketonuria have a number of problems, some of which have yet to be solved. Those who object to the program have focused on these problems, which are dwarfed, in my opinion, by the potential benefits.

We now know that young women who have been treated for phenylketonuria are at great risk for producing defective children, because the treatment for phenylketonuria is ordinarily discontinued when the child is 6 to 8 years of age. Although the blood phenylalanine levels rise to abnormal levels, mental abilities are stable, because of the fact that the central nervous system has developed. Young women who are affected with phenylketonuria and are of normal intelligence, but who have abnormal blood phenylalanine levels, produce defective offspring with structural, as well as mental, disability. This seems attributable to the fact that the developing fetus exists in a markedly abnormal biochemical environment. We thus have a dilemma of what to advise the young woman with phenylketonuria as she nears the reproductive age. Although this is a problem we must work on, I think that no one would seriously recommend that we discontinue treatment to prevent this problem.

Other screening programs are likely to develop. Currently, the most common one under discussion is that for discovering hypothyroidism in the newborn. Hypothyroidism, or thyroid dysfunction in infancy, if not defined early, also leads to significant retardation. A simple, inexpensive screening test is likely to be instituted. Again, this test should be a potential benefit to all on whom it is run, and its potential value seems to far outweigh the risk.

It seems to me that a simple rule of thumb for the screening programs is that they should be simple, not produce significant harm or discomfort to the patient, and be of calculable potential benefit to each person studied. Such guidelines would be practical and helpful in reviewing such programs.

One of the final things to consider is that of experimental treatment in childhood. This is an area in which great judgmental decisions must be made. There are different opinions about what constitutes acceptable risks for certain kinds of treatment. Some experimental treatments go beyond what many would accept. However, I think that most investigators of treatments in childhood would agree considerably about what is an acceptable risk.

I would like to discuss an experimental treatment in which we are involved that involves considerable risk to the patient. We feel that this treatment is justified because the condition with which we are working is extremely severe, uniformly produces substantial brain damage, and is uniformly fatal. The condition is one of a family of diseases known collectively as the mucopolysaccharidoses. In these conditions, mucopolysaccharides accumulate in all the tissues of the body and prominently involve the bones and joints, the heart valves, and the brain tissue. These diseases vary in their mechanism of inheritance (autosomal recessive or X-linked recessive), but are characterized by a series of genetic deficiencies of enzymes normally responsible for degrading mucopolysaccharides. (Mucopolysaccharides are important constituents of ground substance, which is simply the "glue" holding the fibers and other cells together.)

Our experiments are currently focused on the Hunter syndrome, in which an enzyme that causes the lysosomal storage of mucopolysaccharides is deficient. Deficient cells from patients with this syndrome can take up the enzyme from normal cells and correct their defect in the laboratory. Our experiments involve the infusion into an affected patient of normal white blood cells, which are rich in enzyme. This condition is inherited as an X-linked recessive, which means that the gene is transmitted through the mother and clinically affects only males. The father is clinically and enzymatically normal, and has served as a donor for white blood cells. His white cell production is such that large numbers of white cells can be taken from him over a period of days with no detectable change in his total white blood cell count. The white blood cells are then infused into the child, who has had extensive immunologic studies, similar to those that would be done if he were to receive a kidney transplant from his father. The risks of infusing materials like white blood cells in large quantities are largely related to immunologic reactions, such as rejection of the cells.

The 4-year-old child we are studying has been under treatment with infusions for periods of 7 to 8 days at 6-month intervals since about 6 months of age. It is too early to assess the effect of the treatments, although he seems to be doing far better than the average patient at this age. This is suggested by the fact that he has essentially normal development, and is delayed only in the area of hearing and speech, which we feel is at least partly related to the significant ear difficulties he has had.

This is a condition in which the experimental treatment involves significant risk of immediate or long term immunologic reactions and other reactions that might occur with white cell infusion. We have minimized these as far as we can with extensive immunologic studies, carried out under the most sophisticated monitoring and emergency treatment environments. No other known treatment would be of benefit to this child, and there is suggestive evidence that this might be helpful. We have fully explained this to the parents, who have observed untreated family members with this condition. At the time treatment was begun, the experimental treatment decisions were fully those of the parents and the physician. I know of no other way to obtain permission in such situations.

In summary, I have discussed several issues that I consider important in pediatric research and data acquisition in normal children. Mine are the views of a physician who has been involved in clinical research in children throughout his entire career, but who has always worked with families throughout this time. My biases are those of a physician to children, a clinical investigator, and a pragmatist.

Some of the problems presented here have too often been considered by philosophers and ethicists, whose insight into what I perceive as the necessity for clinical invesitgation has been insufficient to permit them to make excellent judgments. On the other side of the coin, clinical investigators have sometimes made decisions many would consider unwise because they are not tempered by the experience of the ethicist and the philosopher or those who are extra-ordinarily sympathetic to the personal needs of children and their parents.

It would seem to me that the new generation of physician/ scientists who have had significant training and experience in ethics will help us bridge this gulf. It is essential that we not be paralyzed in our clinical investigative efforts by the uninformed, but at the same time we must be sensitive to the fact that our studies must consider a host of humanitarian aspects.

THE HUMAN AS EXPERIMENTAL ANIMAL
Necessary or Desirable?

Jan van Eys

An institution like M. D. Anderson Hospital and Tumor Institute is presupposed to be dedicated to clinical research, because its mission is to alleviate human suffering caused by cancer. It should, therefore, zealously seek its self-destruction. But very few individuals can approach the end of their labors with equanimity. This has resulted in a curious dichotomy. On the one hand, hypotheses are tested to satisfy the curiosity of the individual investigator, independent of a specific larger goal. On the other hand, a multi-modal systems approach to solving technological problems with simultaneous attack on as yet unlinked subproblems has been enormously successful, resulting in a research superstructure. Research still needs the ingenuity of individual investigators, but it now has specific aims to solve specific diseases. Therefore, clinical research has become a major approach to medical problem solving.

Clinical research has limitations that health science bench research does not have, because the specific problem under investigation cannot be divorced from human needs. Of course, clinical research can be defined as any research (i.e., any investigation that tests a hypothesis) relating to human biology. It would then include recent spectacular accomplishments, such as the unraveling of the modulation of the oxygen-carrying function of hemoglobin and the consequent understanding of improved tissue oxygen delivery through red cell adaptation to high altitude or chronic anemia; or the discovery and structural determination of the precursor molecule of insulin, proinsulin, and the impact that has had on understanding diabetes. However, this discussion is limited to research that involves the human study of human beings (this phrase is the title of an editorial by

Margaret Mead (*1*)). Such studies assume that the human is the only available experimental animal at that stage of the inquiry.

It is necessary to stress that we are discussing experimentation. Clinical research implies the testing of a hypothesis regarding human biology that includes active intervention by the researcher in the physiology or biochemistry of the subject. We need to examine 1) when such research may be needed, 2) what constitutes good clinical research, which may thereby be justified, and 3) what questions one can hope to answer with this investigational system. Finally, the question of the desirability of employing the human as an experimental animal must be addressed.

GUIDELINES OF RESEARCHER-SUBJECT RELATION

The relationship between human-researcher and human-subject must be specifically defined. The ethics of the relationship are an inseparable consideration in the design of experimentation. Thus, some ethical reflections must be given so the medical framework can be discussed within a proper perspective.

The need for consent by the subject is a given. (The nature of the consent and the definition of informed consent is of course a major problem, in conceptual ferment as is no other area of medicine.) A second demand relates to the need for the experiment. The so-called Nuremburg code asserts, "The experiment should be such as to yield fruitful results for the good of society, unprocurable by other methods or means of study and not random or unnecessary in nature" (*2*). It does not mention the good of the subject. Even the trial of a new drug found beneficial in animal studies in an otherwise hopelessly ill patient is not automatically for the good of the subject, unless a detailed psychological and ontological analysis of the situation is made. The good of society is usually the major determining factor in whether or not an experiment is conducted. Clearly then, a clinical experiment must always be part of an overall plan and only rarely can it assume the ivory tower isolation of the bench experiment.

THE NEED FOR CLINICAL RESEARCH

Our next problem is, what constitutes need for clinical research? Although humans are, in many ways, very poor experimental subjects, they are the most commonly used experimental animals in biomedical research because it is assumed that relevant data on human biology, especially human pathobiology, are more readily obtainable in humans than in other species. That is assumed to be self-evident, but all self-evident hypotheses are suspect. Aristotle thought it self-evident that a large stone would drop faster than a small one, and he never tried the experiment that would have proved him wrong. An experiment in humans should be performed only when the answer cannot be obtained in any model system. To experiment on humans demands the ultimate in scientific thinking, the best one has to offer. Nobel Prize winner Albert Szent-Györgyi stated, "The essential feature of this [scientific] thinking is humility, the realization of our imperfections. The first command of this thinking is to accept nothing without evidence, face problems as such, with a cool head, without fear or prejudice, with uncompromising honesty of thought, unbiased by fear, hopes, or interest" (*3*).

Even when an unbiased examination of the experimental options allows no other animal than the human as experimental subject, that does not automatically ensure good research. Any research, no matter how trivial, requires verifying a hypothesis by experimentation. But even if the hypothesis is valid, the human the only available animal, and the ethics clear, one may still falter. There are many pitfalls:

1. It must be possible to obtain an answer while the question remains reasonable. The classic example is the case of the untreated controls in the study of syphilis recently brought to light in Alabama. As long as therapy was not necessarily better than no therapy, an untreated control was reasonable, but once penicillin was found to be effective, continuation of the experiment was senseless.

    Problems exist in clinical oncological research. The data of the pediatric division of the Southwest Oncology Group (SWOG) cooperative studies on childhood acute lymphocytic leukemia show a gradually increasing median survival (*4*) (Figure 1), but this survival was at one time decidedly inferior to a set of data from St. Jude's Research Hospital (*5*). Because any experiment will take three median survivals, or at least 5 years, to produce meaningful data, there was pressure to abandon sequential development of therapy in favor of the St. Jude's schema. It can become very difficult to make a judgment about when one should be satisfied with other people's results.

2. The experiment must test the hypothesis, and not yield data on accidental perturbation from the expected steady state of the experimental subjects. This perturbation is called the Hawthorne

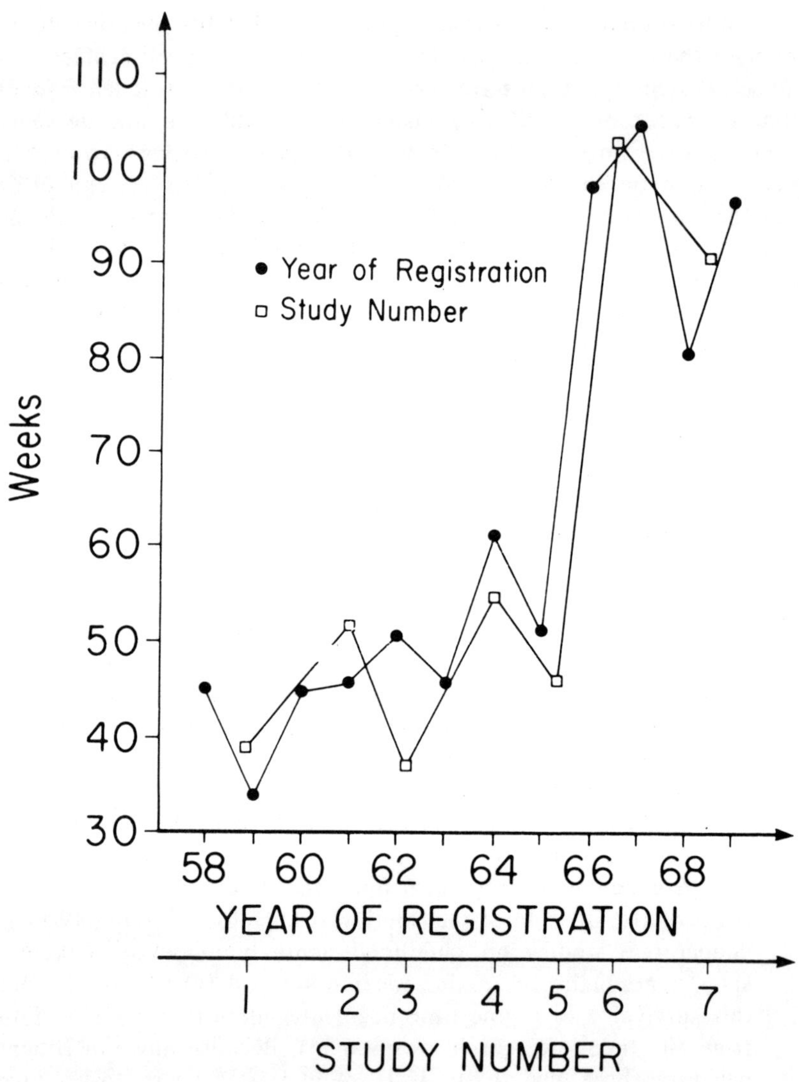

Figure 1.   Median survival by year, as seen in the studies of the Southwest Oncology Group, 1958–1968. (Courtesy of George, S. L., *et al.*: Cancer 32:1547–1553, 1973.)

effect, after experiments carried out at the Hawthorne plant of the Western Electric Company in Chicago during the 1920's and 30's to evaluate the effect of changed working conditions on productivity. The conclusions were that the intense observation of the research process itself resulted in increased productivity (6). The clinical researcher tries to guard against this phenomenon by double-blind studies in which neither patient nor physician knows the variable to be tested at a particular time (*7*). However, there is also the inverse of the Hawthorne effect: the research physician treats his or her patients differently from the way the regular physician does, just as the research rat is the sleekest, healthiest animal. Data from England suggested such a phenomenon when the results of children with acute lymphocytic leukemia treated in centers were compared with those in communities (*8*) (Table 1).

Clearly, the experiment itself is a variable that cannot be controlled; it is this consideration that argues against historical controls. This is also the basis for the thesis that research patients are better off than control patients in therapeutic trials for diseases for which the cure is not yet known (*9*).

3. The measurement must be relevant to the question asked. For example, a recent study summarized data on the use of actinomycin D against Wilms' tumor, and asked whether this drug in a single dose was inferior to a multiple dose regimen. If inferiority was defined in terms of survival, the answer appeared to be "No" (Table 2). However, this was largely misleading because retreatment of the recurrences that happened after the single dose was successful (*10*).

Many more such caveats could be discussed, but these three should exemplify the pitfalls in clinical research.

GOOD CLINICAL RESEARCH

Good clinical research requires a sound hypothesis, tested in the only relevant experimental animal in an ethically justified way, with clearly defined variables. To do clinical research well, one must examine all

Table 1.   Median survival time (in weeks) in acute lymphocytic leukemia in children[a]

Subjects	2–8 years		9–14 years	
	Number cases	Median survival	Number cases	Median survival
Registered cases excluding study group	454	36	145	22
Study group	146	72	19	74

[a] These data are from England and Wales during the years 1963–1967.

Table 2.   Actinomycin D in Wilms' tumor (children's cancer group A)

Subjects	Drug administration	
	Single course	Multiple course
Number of patients		
Enrolled	36	37
Evaluable	28	25
Number surviving	20 (71%)	20 (80%)
Number of relapses	16	7
Number surviving after relapse	8	2

research critically and be wary. In patient care, where therapy is not certain to be curative, codification of approach is much better than individualism, but codification only as long as one learns. Researchers who maintain such disciplines even when they are not experimenting should be sought out.

On the other hand, research that is designed solely to use a specific available tool is suspect. Therefore, any large cooperative clinical trial is suspect; not wrong, but suspect.

Hypotheses must be sequential, not apropos of nothing. However, repeated hypotheses based on somebody else's prior hypotheses become suspect. This is different from repeating, for the sake of confirmation, a spectacular but unexpected result by others.

Originality is a sine qua non: if we could agree before an experiment on the outcome, it would not be a hypothesis. Much research falls into the category of what the Dutch call "kicking in open doors," yet many unwarranted assumptions exist in medicine. Any hypothesis that is based on the assumption of a self-evident truth is suspect.

There are basic techniques in research, just as there are in all bodies of knowledge. Any research that deviates greatly from established experimental design is suspect.

Good clinical research is rare. Some have implied that there is no room for purely applied drug research, what is called clinical pharmacology. However, just as technology makes buildings possible, so clinical pharmacology makes therapeutics possible. Clinical pharmacology is to clinical research what the development of an assay for a metabolite is to the unraveling of a metabolic pathway, but it cannot stand by itself.

To ask trivial questions that require a nontrivial experiment to answer is clearly poor research. Clinical research can be nontrivial, as witnessed by the progress against leukemia. The sequential development of such research can be traced. People asked, "Is leukemia curable?" and the answer seemed to be, "Yes, occasionally." Others then asked, "Can it predictably be done with existing drugs?" and the answer was again thought to be, "Yes." Then some asked, "What was essential in the mixture of drugs that I used?" Then, painstakingly, drug by drug, dosage by dosage, comparisons were made. However, the historical questions made the final comparisons nontrivial. Without that foundation, questions are meaningless.

Publishability is not an infallible criterion of worth: both Drs. Albert Szent-Györgyi and Arthur Kornberg had research papers rejected that later won them Nobel Prizes, and yet the literature is replete with research that is trivial because no fundamental questions are asked.

Although good clinical research can be defined or least recognized, we still have not dealt with the necessity for clinical research. Is human experimentation outside the realm of clinical trials with direct patient benefit or unique human disease ever justifiable? The answer lies in the fact that much good clinical research deals with the single patient, rather than large numbers of subjects.

For the purposes of research, a human is definable on morphological and biological grounds. The phenotype "human" is the consequence of a large number of biochemically active or structurally important proteins. The *function* of such proteins determines the phenotype; the structure of such proteins is only important as it affects function; many possible structural variations do not affect function and therefore are allowable variations within the definition of "human."

Function, however, may be adequate under ordinary circumstances, but inadequate when an extreme challenge occurs. The classic example is glucose-6-phosphate dehydrogenase deficiency. Glucose-6-phosphate dehydrogenase is the first enzyme in a metabolic chain used to maintain red cell integrity. Under ordinary circumstances the red cell is stable, even when the enzyme is somewhat deficient. However, some drugs tend to oxidize the red cell membrane, causing hemolytic anemia. (Many reviews on glucose-6-phosphate dehydrogenase exist. A useful start is by Keller (*11*)). As we learn the primary structures of more and more proteins, we discover more and more variants. We know of over 120 different molecular species of human hemoglobin and over 60 variants of glucose-6-phosphate dehydrogenase. If we extend this variability over 2,000 protein species, the chance of identity between two humans is so small as to be nonexistent except in identical twins. Many decades ago, Dr. R. J. Williams proposed the concept of biochemical individuality before the genetic knowledge of today made this a reasonable hypothesis (*12*).

If clinical research is an experiment that minimizes variables, then the fewer and more closely related the subjects are, the better it is. Thus, the results on one patient are more reliable than those on large groups if detailed metabolic and pathophysiological questions are asked. Large groups allow answers only to simple questions.

It does, of course, happen that a variation in genetic structure results in disturbed metabolism, so that biochemical data can be obtained on humans through what Dr. Robert Good[1] called "experiments of nature" and Dr. A. E. Garrod called "inborn errors of metabolism." Many of our concepts of immunology stem from observations of such patients. Research in such diseases can transcend the study of the disease itself. One of the first inborn errors of metabolism mentioned by Dr. Garrod was pentosuria (*14, 15*). Dr. Oscar Touster unraveled an entire new metabolic pathway that came to light because of the metabolic experiment nature executed in pentosurics (*16*).

It is easy to view a genetic disease as an experiment in nature and to accept the value of studying the patient with a rare disorder in depth. One could argue that a contracted disease, such as a malignancy, falls into a different conceptual category, but it is quite possible to look at such a disease as a challenge to ordinary homeostasis, and therefore as an experiment of nature in its own right.

There are advantages to studying the individual patient over studying the "disease." First, the single patient makes possible diagnostic certainty. This does not mean we know what the diagnosis actually is, only that there is but one diagnosis. Diagnoses in malignant disorders are often highly subjective. I need remind you only of the difficulty in distinguishing acute lymphocytic leukemia from acute granulocytic leukemia of childhood. There is a clinical distinction, but at least one member of the SWOG pediatric division said he could not tell the difference and reported all children as ALNOS (acute leukemia, not otherwise specified). Therefore, when the question in the research relates to the host-disease interaction, one intensively studied patient is far preferable to multiple patients, even if the name given to the tumor is only approximately correct.

---

[1] The many reviews of his work are represented in Reference 13.

Once an experiment has been performed, further active intervention could be actually undesirable. Then the single patient can become a fruitful subject of observation. If one has a thorough knowledge of the disease or the host up to that time, meaningful data can be gained. Such observations, however, presuppose a knowledge of the patient and disease to the largest extent possible.

A clear example of such data gathering can be drawn from a disease with a specific therapeutic dilemma. I would again like to dwell briefly on a genetic disease, largely because the example involves a personal experience. Pyruvate kinase deficiency is a genetic disease that can result in very severe hemolytic anemia (*17*). It is very difficult to ascertain whether or not splenectomy is beneficial. There is little prediction in the usual hemolytic criteria; the hemolysis appears to be intravascular. It occurred to us that the varying results seen with splenectomy were attributable to the fact that the reticulocyte, not the mature red cell, was being removed, because after splenectomy any improvement in circulating hemoglobin could be accounted for by the rise in reticulocyte count. After that, an experiment could be designed. The observation could be readily proved by differential labeling of reticulocytes and mature red cells and by drawing survival curves and doing sequestration studies. Such an experiment could be justified because it helped determine whether or not splenectomy was beneficial in such patients.

It is the single patient who is unique. It is the single human who can be the ideal experimental animal. It is possible to examine the type of nontrivial questions one may ask in good research. This discussion is based on malignant diseases, but analogous reasoning can be made for other diseases.

1. *Etiology*: The ultimate question in any disease is, "What causes it?" Determining what happens in one patient is much easier than examining, for instance, the sera of 100 patients with similar tumors, because of the vagaries of pathology and the variable natural history of malignancies. Tissue culture of a specific tumor cell line from a specific patient with a defined history is much more reliable than from a large number of cell lines from similar patients. Genetic factors do not readily stand out in a study of a large number of patients, but they do in an in-depth study of the immediate kinship of one patient.

2. *Pathophysiology*: Determining what is happening in a given patient's history is often more helpful than reviewing data on many patients.

3. *Therapy*: On occasion there are findings in therapy made clearer by one patient than by large uncontrolled therapeutic trials. The first patient who gets a new drug is the obvious example. Drug data on a few carefully monitored patients are as reliable as, if not more so than, superficial data on 100.

There are a number of examples of research on individual patients relative to oncology from which major findings of general interest have resulted.

1. *Multiple myeloma*: Dr. Frank Putnam pioneered the study of the chemistry of Bence Jones proteins and unraveled the structure, proved its monoclonal origin, and found clues of its relationship to the structure of immunoglobulins (*18*). Since the individual proteins are unique, the structure could only be deduced from the study of individual urines. Pooling would have given no answer.
2. *Pure red cell aplasia*: The association between pure red cell aplasia and thymoma led to the hypothesis that an immunological etiology existed. Because the end point of therapy can only be inducing the patient to make red cells and spontaneous recovery does not occur, the study of individual patients could be used to test the effect of immunosuppressive therapy. By simultaneously growing marrow in vitro, researchers could demonstrate an erythrotoxic antibody and gauge the relationship between the red cell toxicity and therapeutic effect (*19*).
3. *Leukemia*: A 16-year-old girl with acute lymphocytic leukemia who was refractory to conventional therapy was given a marrow transplant from an HLA-matched brother. The graft was successful, but leukemia recurred in 62 days. Cytogenic studies showed that the leukemia that recurred had a male karyotype, and therefore was presumably in the donor cells. The donor to date has not developed leukemia (*20*). The implications are staggering. This result could not have been foreseen and could only have been made clear by individual patient study.

These examples are not the newest nor necessarily the most spectacular ones I could quote. However, good research remains good research even if the question is not world shaking, but only idea modifying.

Must one make a conceptual difference between children and adults as research subjects? Ethically that seems obvious, but medically it is not true. The child is a person with independent rights and privileges, as well as a human with often unique properties. Therefore, the child should have the same access to research as the adult.

THE CONTEXT OF RESEARCH

The argument comes dangerously close to suggesting that the end justifies the means. Defining clinical research as research on humans by humans, we have argued that criteria for testing good clinical research can be set. Clinical research could be directly for the benefit of the patient because therapeutic intent is primary or because genetically the patient is exhibiting unique deviations from the normal. However, we argued that any disease is a perturbation of homeostasis and that, therefore, there is no conceptual difference between genetic and nongenetic human disease. We finally argued that intense study of the single patient often yields superior data. But whereas examples of unique yields of human research were cited, they do not prove that human research is necessary or desirable

Those two criteria, necessity and desirability, are, however, entirely separate. Nothing is necessary unless achieving the goal is considered a necessity. If you really want to learn to control a disease, human experimentation may be needed before in-depth study in an animal model can unravel the details. After all, the model cannot be recognized unless and until a basic understanding of the human disease allows a comparison. Therefore, the question of whether or not experimentation is justified depends on the goal one wants to achieve. The end does justify the means, but the derogatory implication of that phrase is not intended. It only states that necessity is relative, and there are consequences of setting goals.

Whether or not the research is desirable is an ethical question separate from whether or not it is needed. Whether or not the question is urgent enough to be answered in spite of ethical uncertainty is not addressed in this chapter. One cannot argue ethical issues with pragmatic reason. Current medical reasoning is experimental; therefore, it asks for human experimentation. The ethical constraints a physician or patient or society sets on physician-patient interaction reflect concepts of humanism, religion, and family relations totally independent of the logical consequences of a medical scientific stance.

Therefore, the only argument made here concerning the desirability of human research is that the question of the necessity of human research is not trivial and should not automatically be rejected.

Current medical concepts logically lead to human experimentation, not as an unavoidable degeneration, but as a necessity for ultimate control of disease, potentially quite compatible with morally and ethically derived guidelines. However, such guidelines say nothing about the desirability of such experimentation. The medical dimension argues that the human subject is needed. The ethical dimension asks whether or not we should live by medicine alone. We must not confuse these two.

REFERENCES

1. Mead, M. 1961. The human study of human beings. (Editorial). Science 133:163.
2. United States vs. Karl Brandt et al., United States Adjuvant General's Department. Trials of War Criminals Before Nuremberg Military Tribunals, under Control Council Law No. 10 (October 1946–April 1949), Vol. 2, The Medical Case. 1947. pp. 181–183. U. S. Government Printing Office, Washington, D. C.
3. Szent-Györgyi, A. 1963. Lost in the twentieth century. Annu. Rev. Biochem. 32:1–14.
4. George, S. L., Fernbach, D. J., Vietti, T. J., Sullivan, M. P., Lane, D. M., Haggard, M. E., Berry, D. H., Lonsdale, D., and Komp, D. 1973. Factors influencing survival in pediatric acute leukemia. Cancer 32:1547–1553.
5. Aur, R. J. A., and Pinkel, D. 1973. Total therapy of acute lymphocytic leukemia. Cancer 5:155–170.
6. Roethlisberger, T. J., and Dickson, W. J. 1939. Management and the Worker. Harvard University Press, Cambridge.
7. Levine, R. J., and Cohen, E. D. 1974. The Hawthorne effect. Clin. Res. 22(3):111–112.
8. Report to the Medical Research Council from the Committee on Leukaemia and the Working Party on Leukaemia in Childhood: duration of survival of children with acute leukaemia. 1971. Br. Med. J. 4:7–9.
9. Holland, J. F. 1969. Who should treat acute leukemia? JAMA 209:1511–1513.
10. Wolff, J. A., D'Angio, G., Hartmann, J., Krivit, W., and Newton, W. A., Jr. 1974. Long term evaluation of single versus multiple courses of actinomycin D therapy of Wilms' tumor. N. Engl. J. Med. 290:84–86.
11. Keller, D. F. 1971. G-6PD Deficiency. CRC Press, Cleveland.
12. Williams, R. J. 1956. Biochemical Individuality. John Wiley & Sons, Inc., New York.
13. Good, R. A. 1972. Disorders of the immune system. In: R. A. Good and W. Fisher, (eds.), *Immunobiology*, p. 3. Sinauer Association Inc., Stamford, Conn.
14. Garrod, A. E. 1908. Lecture IV. Lancet 2:214.

15. Garrod, A. E. 1923. Inborn Errors of Metabolism. 2nd Ed. Hodder & Stoughton Ltd., London.
16. Touster, O. 1959. Pentose metabolism and pentosuria. Am. J. Med. 26(5):724.
17. van Eys, J., and Garms, P. 1971. Pyruvate kinase deficiency hemolytic anemia: a model for correlation of clinical syndrome and biochemical anomalies. Adv. Pediatr. 18:203–229.
18. Putnam, F. W., Titani, K., Wikler, M., and Shinoda, T. 1967. Structure and evoltuion of kappa and lambda light chains. Cold Spring Harbor Symp. Quant. Biol. 32:9.
19. Krantz, S. B. 1974. Pure red cell aplasia. N. Engl. J. Med. 291(7): 345–350.
20. Fialkow, P. J., Thomas, E. D., Bryant, J. I., and Neiman, P. E. 1971. Leukaemia transformation of engrafted human marrow cells in vivo. Lancet 1:251–255.

ETHICAL QUANDARIES

MORAL AND SPIRITUAL ASPECTS OF RESEARCH ON CHILDREN
An Introduction

Hyman J. Schachtel

It is my privilege as chairman of this session to welcome you here and to introduce the four participants who explore our challenging theme, "The Ethics of Medical Research on Children." We want to know whether or not it is ethical to experiment nontherapeutically with children to find a cure for dreadful maladies. Has society the right to tempt volunteers by material reward to submit to such procedures? Can a child competently make such a decision? Is it right to ask parents to let their child be used for experimentation when physicians cannot be certain of side effects or of later dire developments that may be caused by the treatments?

On the other hand, what of the moral duty of medical researchers to discover how to overcome malignancies that destroy the lives of children and that curse the homes of thousands with despair and suffering? We have only to think of the devastation afflicted by polio on our youngsters just a short time ago. How blessed are we all by the Salk and Sabin vaccines! They have lifted the burden of fear and apprehension from the hearts of the parents of America and the world. They have freed our children at least from this threat to their health and lives.

Ethics, which has to do with the rightness or wrongness of actions, has been defined in many ways by many astute minds. Recently I heard Mr. Ed Haggerty, president of Texas Instruments and chairman of the board of trustees of Rockefeller University, define ethics by saying, "An ethical person is one who does not deliberately hurt another person." I also recall a wonderful older colleague of mine defining ethics in this way: "An ethical person is one who is unable to be comfortable in the presence of another person's discomfort." And then, of course, there is the great statement of the prophet Micah, who said, "What doth the Lord require of Thee? Only to do justly, to love mercy, and to walk humbly with thy God." Here we find ethics involved with justice, with compassion, and with humility. I do not know how our speakers narrow their definitions in order to meet the requirements of our theme, but I do know that this is a subject of tremendous concern and interest.

To experiment or not to experiment on children to discover how to deal effectively with destructive or disabling diseases, that is our question. As a religious teacher, I would like to suggest that the moral and spiritual aspects of this problem must be weighed by the parents. They should take the ultimate responsibility for any decision. The healthy child who protests against any part of the experiment, however, should not be forced to participate. Our participants are highly qualified. We shall hear from Drs. Paul Ramsey, William G. Bartholome, Jerome W. Berryman, and Kenneth L. Vaux.

ETHICAL DIMENSIONS OF EXPERIMENTAL RESEARCH ON CHILDREN

Paul Ramsey

The ethos of research with human subjects differs from country to country. Charles U. Lowe, M.D., Executive Director of the National Commission for the Protection of Human Subjects of Biomedical and Behavioral Research, maintains that Great Britain, unlike the United States, does not permit nontherapeutic research on children. This contrast is frequently denied by others who usually cite a single article by Curran and Beecher (*1*). However, the authors make no mention of the fact that Anglo-American common law with regard to voiceless subjects may be construed as justifying experimentation on comprehending human subjects: an understanding and voluntary consent. Nor do they take into account the difficulty of getting the issue into the stream of case law, or whether the research profession in either country deems that desirable. The Medical Research Council of Great Britain (*2*) evidently believes that "nonbeneficial" pediatric research is prohibited in Great Britain, because, although subscribing to that ban, it introduced a proper latitude in the understanding of "child" for research purposes. The "age of consent" need not be the same as that for other competent consents or for all protocols into which the cooperation of children is admissible.

At a coffee break during a session of the National Commission, I reminded Dr. Lowe that he had stated (or allowed to be stated) in the first proposed guidelines published in the *Federal Register* (*3*) that there is some uncertainty in our law about using children in nontherapeutic research. Doctor Lowe responded that we would soon have a definitive resolution of the issue in the case of Nielsen vs. Regents of the University of California, et al. This suit challenges the use of healthy children in a 5-year prospective study of the development of allergic diseases, and experiments upon unconscious persons who were accepted in an unconscious state for care as patients. In the latter case, the procedures had nothing to do with emergency first aid care and are alleged not to have been intended for the patient's benefit.

When it is said that there is confusion in the law regarding nontherapeutic pediatric research, what is meant is that the common law says one thing whereas the contrary is stated by the Federal Food and Drug Administration, which maintains that no drug can be marketed for the treatment of diseases unless it has first been tested for safety and efficacy in human beings.[1] In the case of uniquely pediatric diseases, that would seem to require testing in children who are not ill. The argument is that limiting such testing to children who are ill with the disease for which the drug is intended would retard pediatric research and, moreover, that controlled clinical trials[2] using normal children are necessary for truly scientific testing, and often field trials for adequate testing. Yet in law an unconsented touching is assault and battery, not only a harmful touching or one that intends harm.

I am not unmindful of the bind in which pediatric research finds itself between the mission to bring aid by the conquest of pediatric diseases and the obligation to protect the child-subject from harm and to respect the human character of the subject by acknowledging that only an authentic consent warrants any touching of the body not in that person's interests. Indeed, I dwell in the same quandary between what is "good" and what is "right." So I do not address this work-shop with any hope of persuasion. Ethos determines what is felt and done more than ethical reasoning does; indeed, ethos is another word for an accepted practice. And there can be no doubt that our American research ethos favors experimentation on children (however reluctantly). The consensus of such a workshop as this might be dif-

---

[1] Also Federal Food, Drug and Cosmetic Act, Section 505 (i): "experts using such drugs for investigational purposes [must] certify to such manufacturer or sponsor that they will inform any human beings to whom such drugs, or any controls used in connection therewith, are being administered, *or their representatives*, that such drugs are being used for investigational purposes and will obtain the consent of such human beings *or their representatives*" (italics added). For background and discussion see reference 4.

[2] See reference 5 for a superb and telling demonstration of the abrogation of fully sensitive medical judgment if physicians enter even patients needing treatment into a control clinical trial of two drugs or procedures.

ferent in Great Britain. I must follow moral reasoning—or at least my best attempts at moral reasoning—wherever it leads, even if it goes contrary to accepted practice. The most I hope to do is to place some thought-provoking considerations alongside the premises of current pediatric research practice. I do not expect to upset the going research ethos or to derail anyone's conclusions.

For a beginning, perhaps we can agree that it is not enough simply to stipulate that parental or guardian consent can be substituted for a voiceless subject's own consent. An ethicist would not have been invited to address this interdisciplinary workshop if substitution by mere stipulation were to be kept from examination. I shall not rehearse lines of argument I have made in the past, that are already in the public forum (*4, 6–9*). Instead, I want to draw your attention to some significant respects in which we twist and squirm—precisely because physician-researchers are moral people—in the course of justifying the use of children in nonbeneficial experimentation. My endeavor is simply to cause a reasonable amount of commotion.

First of all, two additional stipulations must sustain the stipulation that the children must be in some need before parents deliberately place them in any danger: 1) the children must be used in research only for the sake of other children and 2) the experimentation must entail minimal or no risk. These two stipulations support one another as well as the first.

Ponder now the routine, cliché, almost ritualistic repetition of that expression "minimal risk." I can most rapidly make my point by a series of quotations from the deliberations on fetal research by the National Commission. The remarks apply also to pediatric research.

One commissioner, Karen Lebacqz, called attention to the evaluative nature of the term "minimal risk," and suggested at least a note that "we are aware of the fact that it is a judgmental term" (*10*). In the ensuing discussion, "noninvasive" and "no additional risk" were mentioned as possible meanings, as well as "so minimal as to be immaterial" and "no conceivable harm." In the discussion of nontherapeutic research on the pregnant woman, Commissioner Lebacqz spoke to the point again. "I notice that the term 'minimal risk' has been used. I would like to know," she asked, "if that term has been defined in the document. If not, I am going to have problems with it," and she observed, "I find the term 'minimal risk' to be almost a void term." Robert E. Cooke tried to quiet objections by stating that "it is commonly accepted"; others said it was "standard" language. Albert H. Jonsen felt that although "we are using standard language . . . somebody is going to have to spell it out a little bit more in the body of the report."

Nobody did. Here surely was unfinished business; but why were the commissioners disturbed by their own routine use of a standard expression? I suggest that the reason was that minimal risk has self-executing meaning in medical judgment in the two language contexts from which it is drawn. In treating patients, the meaning of minimal risks is measured against a medical detriment to be prevented. Minimal risk means "acceptable" risk, even acceptable actual harm, balanced by a benefit delivered to or greater harm prevented in the same patient. Likewise, in the research context, the meaning of minimal risk can be determined by the informed consent of normal volunteers; at whatever level set abstractly by the protocol or by the accepted meaning of minimal.

In the case of experimental research on children there is no such limitation, either from consideration of a balance of risks to be borne and benefits to be gained by the single patient or from a normal volunteer's consent to risks he is willing to bear for the medical good of others. Instead, minimal risk to the child-subject is weighed against the benefits for many other children in the minds of surrogates. The commissioners feared that the meaning of minimal risk might be strained when measured against the greater good for many, unless that common standard was more narrowly defined for research purposes.

That proved impossible, not because of the inquisitiveness or acquisitiveness of researchers, but because another interpretation of minimal risk appears whenever children are used in a nontherapeutic experimentation. The welfare of children as a class is the sole stated reason for using child-subjects; other children are the beneficiaries. If the pediatric illness to be conquered is a serious and widespread disease, the research benefit may be deemed sufficient to raise the level of justifiable risk to the subjects. That, after all, is the sole consideration against which to weigh the substituted consent of parents or guardians, not benefit to the child-subjects. The welfare of children as a class could be given higher priority than parental protection of a child. If the expected welfare were very great, the risk to the subjects that could be justified would correspondingly increase. Thus, there is no self-limitation upon the meaning of minimal risk.

However, the worried commissioners never defined the standard more closely. Karen Lebacqz (joined by Albert H. Jonsen) expressed doubt about the usefulness of that stipulation in the context of nontherapeutic research. She pointed out that the risks are always unknown; a routine use of the accepted wording might simply deceive researchers and parents alike into supposing that a really protective limitation was being effectively applied. She urged that caution be exercised "to avoid the temptation to consider the risks to be 'minimal' when in fact they cannot be fully assessed." She went on to say, "I am reluctant to allow any research on the living human fetus [read: uncomprehending child-subject] unless provision has been made for adequate compensation of subjects injured during research."

Thus, the stipulation that substituted consent, transposed from treatment to experimental research, can protect children must rely on the further stipulation that the risks imposed on nonconsenting subjects must be minimal. When that fails—either because the risks are always unknown or because a small chance of great harm is still a grave risk—a second position must be prepared: compensation for untoward or unsuspected injury. To think of compensation shows that the net of protection thrown around uncomprehending subjects (by stipulating minimal risks) is exactly that: a net with holes in it, however small or few, through which slips actual harm. Indeed, schemes of compensation are based on the expectation that minimal risks will not protect from all harm.

No parent should knowingly consent to that. Compensation is the name of the little girl in the crowd at the parade who shouts out loud that King Substituted-Consent, in the case of experimental research on children, is naked. If anyone feels I am waxing rhetorical, I ask you to consider how you would go about fully explaining (to parents whose child you wish to recruit into research having no relation to his or her own welfare) the following two things simultaneously: 1) the research entails "minimal or no risk" to their child, and so and so is the great good you hope to accomplish; and 2) in case their child is injured (which you do not expect), the following is the financial recompense, so many thousands of dollars for the child's lifetime for this, another numbered thousands of dollars for that, etc. I do not deny that some proxy consents may be forthcoming under these circumstances. If this occurs more frequently among parents in the medical and scientific community generally, it may be because they have acquired tastes different from those of ordinary parents. In any case, a researcher's willingness to try an experiment on his or her own children is quite consistent with a willingness to use children for an alien purpose, at possible risk, and with no benefit to the children.

The conclusion is that a need or interest on the part of the child-subjects must be discovered if substituted consent has moral warrant. Without that, or without sufficiently competent supplementary consent on the part of the subject accepting the risk, the responsibility of parenthood would be flawed or deflected from its primary role. A system of compensation would not correct this deflection. Instead, it points to an irremovable weakness in the moral argument for nontherapeutic research on children.

My second point is closer to the center of efforts to give good moral reasons for experimental research on children. If someone reasons that it is immoral to use voiceless children in experimentation having no relation to their own benefit, the rejoinder often is: "It is also immoral not to do pure research on children." By this an appeal is made to the frightful cost to children treated every day by drugs or procedures anecdotally verified or insufficiently tested. By slowing pediatric research, it is said, we are "harming" those who suffer and die from childhood diseases for which there is little or no remedy.

As an ethicist, I know the moral meaning of the word "imperative" in the shorthand expression "the research imperative." It is a good word, summarizing a multitude of positive moral duties to persons in need of present and future medical help. Still, an ethicist needs to know, and a physician-researcher should be prepared to give some reasoned account of, the different weights to be assigned to the imperative to bring aid through research and the imperative to do no harm. Some current research practice—at least statements such as "it is also immoral not to do research on [well] children"—equilibrates these two imperatives, creating a false collision between moral claims, in which ambiguity practice proceeds as dictated by FDA regulations and our American research ethos.

However, an unexamined research ethic is not worth having. Furthermore, it is a fairly well established conclusion in both theological and philosophical ethics that primacy can be assigned to one imperative so it overrides the other in case of conflict. Of the two precepts in the preamble to the natural law (for those who do ethical analysis in that tradition), "do good" has less stringency than "avoid evil," even though good is better. Those two injunctions do not point to obligations having equal weight. When push comes to shove in an apparent conflict, the second has priority over the first. We are to do all the good we morally can, not simply all the good we can. We are to do all the good we can without doing wrong.

The same lexical ordering is often stated in other philosophical languages. Even assuming benevolence to be the motive in both cases, the duty to do no actions that are maleficent is stronger than the duty to accomplish beneficient deeds. Negative obligations are stronger, more universal, and admit no or fewer exceptions than positive obligations. Positive duties are duties of imperfect obligation, whereas negative duties are duties of perfect obligation. Whichever language is used, the conclusion is that we do not have an equally important duty to help people as to refrain from injuring them or from wrongfully using them.

It would be foolhardy to claim that there is complete agreement on this point among ethicists, but I will say this: any "bioethicist" who disagrees with this position in general ethics and who addresses a workshop such as this without exposing his or her general ethical reasons for disagreement with the resolution I have just summarized succeeds only in guaranteeing that he never went to an interdisciplinary conference.

One cannot do without a proper rank ordering of obligations to prevent evil and obligations to beneficence. In this medical ethics is only—and should strive to be nothing other than—a species of general ethics. The truth that to bring aid is a less important requirement than to do no harm accounts for the primacy given the latter principle in traditional medical ethics. Anyone should know that to bring aid is better, and also that we should strive to harmonize bringing aid with doing no harm. However, in a case of irresolvable conflict, it is clear which duty should give way. We are to do all the good we morally can; that is all.

To do no harm is a universal prescription in medical ethics; to bring aid is medicine's constant task. Hans Jonas is quite correct on this point (*11*). Our descendants, he writes, have a right to an unplundered planet; otherwise we do them harm. However, they

> "do not have a right [an imperative moral claim] to new miracle cures. . . . We have not sinned against them if by the time they contract arthritis, it has not yet been conquered (unless by sheer negligence). . . . We can expect ever again the upwelling of a will to give what nobody— neither society, nor fellow man, nor posterity—is entitled to."

As for medicine's constant task, "no one has the shred of a right [i.e., an exactable moral claim] to expect or ask these things. They come to the rest of us as gratia gratis data." Bringing aid cannot be turned into an exactable duty having parity with "do no harm."

Under the spell of promising research benefits, the disparity between these two principles becomes obscure. By verbal slight of hand, we turn failure to bring aid (or having no aid to bring) into doing harm. Parity between the two principles is thereby established. When the two have united, they bring forth the pediatric research dilemma. Yet the truth of the moral judgment expressed in the foregoing analysis of the priority of doing no harm is still at work in our decisions. This lends force to the stipulation "minimal or no risk" with which the voiceless subject is surrounded and to the persuasiveness of incidence-of-risk figures. It also explains our reluctance to have those veils torn aside by confronting candidly proposed schemes of compensation or by acknowledging that the one chance in 3,000 or in 20,000 of a child's death or brain damage under anesthesia is still a grave risk. We first promote the failure to bring aid to equivalence or near equivalence with the wrong of doing harm. Then not all possibility of immediate harm need be excluded from a decision that brings aid. Thus we manage to reconcile possible harm with the responsibilities of parenthood to protect the child, and to validate proxy consent based on no need or interest discoverable in the child.[3]

Dr. William G. Bartholome has attempted to locate such an interest consistent with parenthood (*12*). He suggests that experimentation with children is justified if it is an ingredient in their moral education. I entirely agree with him. That may be a creative direction to go in a consensual society, once we block the way to using uncomprehending subjects for a purpose entirely alien to them.

One caveat only: Bartholome couples the child's moral nurture with "no risk" research, except in one "guideline" that permits "no greater risk or discomfort than would be encountered in family life." This is an ambiguity, standard in all the literature, that should be removed. It could mean doubling the risk or it could mean no more risk. Let the standard be, for example, that an Ideal Mathematician (to be designated by the Secretary of HEW) figure that the risk added while the child is a partner with his or her parents in experimental research is balanced by the omitted risk of a fracture from playing baseball with them during the same period of time.

Of course, no parent engages in such calculations. Still, something like that would abstractly have to be the test. Otherwise parents

---

[3] I am the first to grant that the consequences of this movement in pediatric research ethics are likely to be small in comparison with those in the ethics of neonatal intensive care. There, too, the stringency of doing no harm is under assault, and bringing aid is being redefined as doing harm. Thus, to continue the lives of some infants comes to mean doing them harm, and the novel concept of "the injury of continued existence" gains governance in the care of defective newborns. That will be an entirely different practice from "letting die," which has always been a part of good medicine.

would be meaning to diminish to some degree their protection, making their children "therapeutic orphans" to that added degree of risk for the sake of other indeterminate children whom they to that degree "adopt"; a step in the direction of the merged sociality of Plato's guardian class, where everyone was everybody's parent and nobody a child, in the full sense, of any two guardians. The linkage with moral education removes the stigma of lessening fidelity to one's child. Parental responsibility may thus be better exhibited. That is the principal point. However, it does not remove the incompatibility that may remain between parental protection and deliberately increasing risk of harm. We need to explore whether or not this is so.

Moreover, the Cardon study of research-related injuries (*13*) found that "the risks of participation in [all] nontherapeutic research may be no greater than those of everyday life." So Bartholome's fine proposal needs further elaboration and refinement for moral nurture to be a sufficient benefit coupled with adequate protection to validate using doubtfully consenting subjects in nontherapeutic research.

In passing, let me note that to locate research on children within parental upbringing discloses its limitation to pediatric research to be, at most, a welcomed stipulation, and one whose rationale may be questioned. Bartholome's suggestion has, then, the following added advantage. It helps us parse the proposal that children be used only for research on uniquely childhood diseases. To be sure, such a limitation affords protection, but by an extrinsic stipulation only. All lines of ethical reasoning that I have examined in support of nontherapeutic research on children seem to me, if valid, to show a child's interest in more than the welfare of other children. The same will be true of arguments yet to be advanced. This is clearly the case in Bartholome's proposal. For if a child loves his or her grandmother at least as much as his or her peers, I see no reason why that child may not be entered as a partner in geriatric research. Might not such a venture equally enhance the child's moral sensitivity and be deemed a better course of moral nurture? Of course, nonrational boundaries are to be cherished if they are clearly visible, easily agreed to, or presently accepted. Still, even if other geriatric research subjects are available, why should we deny a child the right to help his or her grandmother, or remove that way to moral maturity?

Still, Bartholome means "no risk"; unlike most apologists who try to define "minimal" risks as "no more than those of daily life." His fine proposal can best be understood in the following way. Attention is taken off of the quantification of risks in parent-child relations, and placed on the meaning of parenthood, on what parents mean to do with their child. Parents hope to further their child's moral education in joint research ventures, just as they hope to further his or her physical and social education by entering him or her into little league baseball. If harm results, that was not their primary purpose. So there need be no quantitative comparison, addition or subtraction, of the risks of these activities in order to determine whether or not they aim to be good parents.

Ethics is no guard against stupidity, nor does it forestall tragedy. At bottom, morality is not a matter of suppressing bad consequences. It has to do with the rectitude of our wills in the discharge of responsibilities in the roles and relations of life. The purpose of parenthood is to protect and nurture. A parent who intends that is doing right, even if he or she is unwise. A physician's role is to protect and save life by medical means. A doctor who intends that is doing right, even if mistakes are made that have dire consequences. Other aspects of medical training are designed to protect the patient from those bad results; and, of course, to be prudent is another aspect of morality. In the case of a researcher, protocol design balances desired consequences with possible harms, and in the case of normal volunteers, the consent requirement provides another check upon a researcher's overreaching.

In discussing pediatric research, we ought always to speak of parental and guardian consent and of the state as parens patriae, and cease to use role-free terms like "proxy," "substitute," or "surrogate." This would put in proper focus—as Bartholome has done—the question of whether or not and under what circumstances a parent or guardian can validly consent to research in behalf of the child. Charles Fried has shown that a physician qua physician cannot enter a patient into a control clinical trial without some diminishment of his care.[4] I suggest that the same is true of proper parental care. Consistent with that is Bartholome's elegant suggestion that research can be fun.

The point in parental consent concerning a child's treatment, or research genuinely related to his or her possible treatment, is the fidelity of parenthood. That is also the point in guardian consent and in the state's interventions as parens patriae when parents fail. As Cardoza said of "joint-adventurers" or "co-partners," so in the case of trustees of every sort: they owe "the duty of the finest loyalty . . . the punctilio of an honor most sensitive" (*14*). The point is simply that

---

[4] Medical bureaucrats, of course, may require that exact records be kept, and thus mount a scientifically controlled observation of the comparative benefits of two different therapies over which conscientious physicians disagree.

parents, guardians, and physicians are trustees, deputies acting for those unable to act in their own right. Only if one discovers some medical interest in treatment or research for a particular child, or some grounds in the moral nurture of the child or capacity in the child to give supplementary consent (which Bartholome believes exists at a quite early age), can consent be given to experimental research with the child without doing violence to the deputyship of parents and guardians. It is not enough to ascribe an inherent "sociability" to the child or "reasonableness" measured by adult standards, or to base surrogate consent on the truth of the proposition that these attributes are inherent in children but not yet exercised. The deputyship of parenthood includes the duty to bring these out, but not to act as if such volitions toward beneficence were already actualized.[5]

REFERENCES

1. Curran, W. J., and Beecher, H. K. 1969. Experimentation in children. JAMA 210:77–83.
2. Medical Research Council. 1964. Responsibility in investigations on human subjects. Br. Med. J. 2(5402):179.
3. Federal Register, 38:221, Nov. 16, 1973, pp. 31740–31742.
4. Ramsey, P. 1970. The Patient as Person, pp. 44–47. Yale University Press, New Haven.
5. Fried, C. 1974. Medical Experimentation, Personal Integrity and Social Policy. North-Holland Publishing Co., Amsterdam.
6. Ramsey, P. 1973. Medical progress and canons of loyalty to experimental subjects. Proceedings of Conference on Biological Revolution/Theological Impact, St. Louis, Missouri. April 6–8. pp. 51–77.
7. Ramsey, P. 1976. Some rejoinders. J. Religious Ethics 4(2):185ff 5ff.
8. Ramsey, P. 1976. The enforcement of morals: nontherapeutic research on children. Hastings Cent. Rep. 6(4):21–30.
9. Ramsey, P. 1977. Children as research subjects: a reply. Hastings Cent. Rep. 7(2):40–41. April.
10. National Technical Information Service. 1975. Transcript of the Sixth Meeting, April 25–26, 1975. p. 560. National Technical Information Service, United States Department of Commerce, Springfield, Va.

---

[5] Nor need one assume a child to be naturally selfish. Notice also that Bartholome's line of reasoning, if it is sound, turns biologic "nonbeneficial" research into participation in biologic research that is beneficial to the child-subject. The word "participation" has human meaning and—unlike most usages today—does not incoherently defend a child's right to be a part. For this reason, such research would fall within the ambit of parental consent. Other efforts to locate a need or interest in the child-subject sufficient to ground valid parental or guardian consent fail. Most notable in the current literature are the articles by Richard A. McCormick, S. J. (*15–17*). See references 5–9 for citations of my articles in rejoinder to McCormick.

11. Jonas, H. 1969. Philosophical reflections on experimentation on human subjects. Daedalus 98:219–247.
12. Bartholome, W. G. 1976. Parents, children, and the moral benefits of research. Hastings Cent. Rep. 6(6):44–45.
13. Cardon, P. V., Dommel, F. W., Jr., and Trumble, R. R. 1976. Injuries to research subjects: a survey of investigators. N. Engl. J. Med. 295: 650–654.
14. Meinhard vs. Salmon, 249 N.Y. 458, 164 N.E. 545 (1928).
15. McCormick, S. J. 1974. Proxy consent in the experimental situation. Perspect. Biol. Med. 18(1):2–20.
16. McCormick, S. J. 1976. Experimentation in children: sharing in sociability. Hastings Cent. Rep. 6(6):41–46.
17. McCormick, S. J. 1976. Experimental subjects: who should they be? JAMA 235:2197–2198.

CENTRAL THEMES IN THE DEBATE OVER INVOLVEMENT OF INFANTS AND CHILDREN IN BIOMEDICAL RESEARCH
A Critical Examination

William G. Bartholome

I would like to focus attention on three recurrent themes in the debate about the involvement of infants and children in research: 1) what has been called "the research imperative," 2) the concept of proxy consent, and 3) the question of benefits, especially to the research subject. However, I must point out that we are addressing these issues not because a few unscrupulous research scientists have conducted a few questionable projects involving infants and children. Those of us who are involved in a critical examination of the involvement of children in research are not radical zealots using a few isolated cases of questionable research projects to stir up trouble for the research community. Infants and children are being systematically exposed to risks in clinical research in almost every major medical center in this country. The pediatric literature reports such instances on a regular basis (*1, 2*). The involvement of normal infants and children in clinical research is widely accepted within the medical community as essential. Parents are being asked and are granting their consent to the involvement of normal infants and children in a wide variety of research projects involving considerable risks.

Already you have heard my fellow presenters claim that the involvement of infants and children in research is imperative. Modern medical practice is rendered virtually impossible unless the research community continues its work. Progress from our present state of knowledge would be impossible. The good practice of medicine demands that research be done. Yet in spite of the overwhelming evidence that such claims are valid, the research enterprise cannot go forward unless people are willing to become participants. The medical community sees itself as obligated to do research. Some have argued that, as members of society, living in interdependence, we all are morally obligated to participate in biomedical research to some extent. However, no one is willing to demand that involvement, to claim that the obligation to do research is so stringent that unwilling subjects should be conscripted. In some sense, then, it can be argued that, in this society, biomedical research is a gratuitous undertaking. The knowledge to be gained is seen as good, but not so essential that our society would collapse without it.

Those who have preceded me have presented a good case for the claim that the practice of pediatric medicine demands on-going research. However, hidden in such a claim is a question. Is it imperative that children be involved in both therapeutic and nontherapeutic research? I am willing, on the basis of what we have heard, to grant the former. But I do not feel that anyone has demonstrated that it is essential to the practice of medicine that children be involved in nontherapeutic research. It would clearly make research much easier, it would clearly improve the pace of research, but I do not believe we have enough evidence to demonstrate that it is essential. The "research imperative" is not an adequate basis on which to argue that infants and children can be justifiably involved in nontherapeutic clinical research.

A second major focus in most of the bioethical literature on the involvement of children in research is on the concept of proxy consent. The reason for this is obvious. Most of those who are working in the field of medical ethics have used a doctrine of consent as a keystone for a theory of medical ethics. This approach was used by my fellow panelist Dr. Paul Ramsey in his widely read book *The Patient as Person* (3). The new journals in medical ethics publish articles on consent in almost every issue. Consent to medical intervention or to involvement in biomedical research is seen not only as a legal issue, not only as good medicine, but also as of central importance in medical ethics.

Ramsey points out that consent is "expressive of the canon of loyalty," of the "faithfulness" of the doctor to the patient or research subject. It indicates that the participants in medical decision making are free, responsible persons. By demanding the consent of the patient to medical intervention, we express our belief that patients are capable of making their own choices and of choosing responsibly (4). Consent is also seen as protective of the interests, health, and freedom of the patient/subject. By making consent a critical moral ingredient, we allow the individual who is in the best position to know those interests to protect them. Also, consent is seen as protecting the physician/investigator from the crushing moral and legal weight of total responsibility. By placing the decision in the hands of the patient/subject, the physician/investigator can share the responsibility.

Although I am willing to argue that the concept of consent has had to carry too much weight in the health care context, my purpose here is to point out to you and to those who are working in medical ethics that many of us, both physicians and investigators, are not involved in relationships with free, responsible patient/subjects. Many of us have to attempt to respond to the needs of patients who cannot consent to our interventions.

The legal system has developed, and those dealing with medical ethics have adopted, a highly pragmatic and usually quite effective solution to this problem; the concept of proxy consent. Little is changed in the doctrine of consent; it is merely shifted from the patient/subject to a parent, guardian, or next-of-kin. I would like to propose that we have accepted and used this concept because it was seen as an attractive and reasonable way out of a dilemma, but that it is an unacceptable concept from a moral point of view. I would ask that we see the concept for what it is, a trap from which we must painstakingly remove ourselves for the sake of our children and those members of our community who are dependent on us. The concept has, by and large, served us well. We may even decide to retain it as a legal device. However, hidden in the concept is what I would term a tyrannical or dehumanizing assumption, that one human being can know another human being so intimately that he or she can know what is right or wrong, good or bad, for that individual. Hidden in this concept is the assumption that infants and children are "morally transparent" to their parents or guardians.

In our society, the concept of proxy consent has been seen and used as a mechanism to protect the so-called right of parents to raise their children as they see fit. It has been used as a means by which parents or guardians were identified as having the right to make decisions for the child. We seem willing to accept the fact that all adults have some responsibility for the children of our society; but parents and guardians have not only been delegated greater amounts of responsibility, they have been given "trump cards," ultimate control, over the lives of their children. The result has been that many parents, particularly of young children, see and respond to them as particularly charming and valuable pieces of property.

I would like to propose that consent to a medical intervention or research project provided by proxy cannot be seen as or responded to in the same way as that provided by an autonomous, responsible decision-maker. To accept them as equivalent is to do violence to children and their status in our society. To refer to them with the same word hides the significant differences.

A classic example of the tyrannical nature of the concept of proxy consent is provided by Father Richard McCormick in a widely read essay, "Proxy Consent in the Experimental Situation" (5). In an attempt to undermine the position of Paul Ramsey that the involvement of children in nontherapeutic clinical research cannot be ethically justified, McCormick argues that Ramsey has failed to address the critical question: why is parental consent considered null in nontherapeutic research whereas it is accepted when procedures are therapeutic? McCormick then proceeds to "unpack" the concept of proxy consent. He argues that proxy consent for therapy is morally valid insofar as it is "a reasonable presumption of the child's wishes, a construction of what the child would wish could he consent for himself." Why? According to McCormick, the obvious answer is that he would choose this if he were capable of choice because he ought to do so. McCormick proceeds to argue that we know infants would choose to be involved in "no discernible risk" clinical research that offers hope of great benefit to others because they, like all of us, ought to be involved in such research, i.e., are obligated to do this as members of the human community.

McCormick's argument has not only been well received by the research community and many medical ethicists, but has had a major impact on the deliberations of the National Commission for the Protection of Human Subjects in Biomedical and Behavioral Research. It has also set off a chain of responses and counterresponses in the literature (6–8). What does it mean to consent? To consent means to "feel with." Included within the capacity to consent is the capacity to see what is being considered, to know what is involved, and to feel what the intervention would mean to oneself. When I give my consent, I make a statement not only about what is being proposed, but about myself. By giving consent, I say that what is proposed is right for me, it fits me and my understanding of myself, my needs, my opinions, beliefs, desires, etc. Consent is a statement about self. Consent is the act of an individual will, a statement about personal willingness. When I provide my consent, I am saying, "I agree, approve, give my permission." To make such a highly personal statement for another involves doing violence to that other. We cannot see, know, and feel for another to this extent. To pretend that we can, to operate as if this were a possibility, is the ultimate in pretentiousness.

As I wrote this, the pediatrician and father in me became very frustrated and impatient and demanded a hearing: "Yes, we agree. But infants and children cannot take care of their own needs. They depend on us to make these decisions for them." Obviously, we must provide for our infants and children. They get sick, and when they do, someone has to take care of them. Some infants and children get so sick that they require medical intervention and their parents usually bring them to the attention of a health care provider.

However, I think that those who examine the interaction between child, parents, and provider from a legal or other abstract perspective fail to see what happens in the tripartite relationship. Consent as a formal legal or moral requirement can be forced on this relationship, but it rarely arises spontaneously. When it does arise, it is seen as a particularly contrived aspect of the interaction. What happens is that the parents relate their observations, feelings, fears, etc., to the physician. He or she will often ask for other observations or information. The patient is then examined. After a period of time in which more information is sought and some thinking is done, the physician will communicate his or her findings and beliefs about the nature of the child's problem and propose a course of intervention. The parents are asked to consider this from their perspective and assent or refuse to assent to the proposed intervention. They do not make a statement about their willingness vis-à-vis the proposed intervention. They make a statement about the appropriateness of the proposed intervention for the child. Such a statement is based only on assumptions about the needs of the child.

Infants and children cannot consent to medical intervention, and no one can know them well enough to consent for them. Infants, in particular, are profoundly unknowable. What parents and health care professionals can do is attempt to respond to children's needs, fully aware of their own ignorance of who the children are and what they might want done for them. To talk of what they would want or what they should want or what they ought to want is to do violence to them as individuals. When we deal with adult members of our society, we can and do talk about "what they would" and "what they should." However, we are talking about people who have a highly developed sense of self and other, who are aware, active, autonomous, and responsible. It is even possible, in the case of those with whom we have been involved in intimate relationships over time, to have a reasonably complete picture of what they would or should want; but even in those most intimate relationships, we leave our feelings and beliefs about "what they would or should" open to their correction or modification. We respect them as persons to this degree!

I am asking that we respect infants and children as developing persons. What warrants our intervention into their lives is not our thesis about what they would or should want. What warrants our involvement is that they stand in need of our help, our care. As William May has argued, what justifies our intervention is that it is undertaken in the hope that it will respond to the demonstrable needs of the infant or child (9). We have no right to intervene. We have an obligation to respond to needs. To act on the basis of assumptions, in the midst of ignorance, is only justifiable if there is some necessity that we act. Because we live in a society in which human activity is undertaken within a legal framework, it is necessary that the parent assent to the proposed response. However, by assenting, by allowing intervention into the life of the child, the parent does not consent to the proposal for the child. When the child is old enough to be aware of self and to communicate his or her feelings and beliefs, we can begin to talk about consent.

The capacity to consent, to feel willing to act in a certain way, is probably present in an embryonic form at what was traditionally referred to as the "age of reason." The child becomes aware of self and the existence of others. I have argued, against Ramsey, that at this age and until late adolescence, a child might justifiably be involved in "no discernible risk" nontherapeutic clinical research with his or her parents (10). I reject the notion that such involvement is obligatory for the child, but I feel that the child and parents might select this activity as one that could enhance the moral development of the child, just as it is morally justifiable for parents and their children to elect to become involved in dancing, music, church activities, little league baseball, etc.

A set of guidelines I have proposed for such involvement, are reviewed here. First, I would like to point out that the justification for such involvement is both the willingness of the child subject and the need for the child to develop as a person. Parents are allowed to let their children be involved with them if the project involves no discernible risk to the health or well-being of the child and if the child sees the activity as good or desirable. Then the child can be said to benefit from the involvement. He or she will not derive medical benefit (narrowly defined), but may benefit in terms of personal growth. To complete these remarks, I have proposed a list of criteria for the involvement of children 5 to 14 years of age in "no discernible risk" clinical research.

1. Meticulous experimental protocol is subjected to institutional peer review
2. Experiment would provide significant and essential new knowledge
3. The knowledge to be gained by the experiment can only be obtained by experimentation involving children
4. The experiment involves no discernible risk or significant discomfort
5. Where possible, the same or a similar experiment has been performed on adult subjects and been found to be without risk
6. Informed parental consent is mandatory. Parents must be involved as experimental subjects with their children where possible. Parental supervision is mandatory where this is not possible
7. The consent of the child subject must be obtained by a member of the research team and by an independent subject-representative
8. The research is reviewed and supervised by an institutional protection committee that includes children in this age range.

REFERENCES

1. Modanlou, H., Yeh, S.-Y., Siassi, B., and Hon, E. H. 1974. Direct monitoring of arterial blood pressure in depressed and normal newborn infants during the first hour of life. J. Pediatr. 85:553–559.
2. Osathanondh, R., Tulchinsky, D., Kamali, H., Fencl, M. deM., and Taeusch, H. W., Jr. 1977. Dexamethasone levels in treated pregnant women and newborn infants. J. Pediatr. 90:617–620.
3. Ramsey, P. 1970. Consent as a canon of loyalty with special reference to children in medical investigations. In: The Patient as Person. pp. 1–58. Yale University Press, New Haven.

4. Freedman, B. 1975. A moral theory of consent. Hastings Cent. Rep. 5:32–39.
5. McCormick, R. A. 1974. Proxy consent in the experimental situation. Perspect. Biol. Med. 18:2–21.
6. Ramsey, P. 1976. The enforcement of morals: nontherapeutic research on children. Hastings Cent. Rep. 6:21–30.
7. McCormick, R. A. 1976. Experimentation in children: sharing in sociality. Hastings Cent. Rep. 6:41–46.
8. McCormick, R. A. 1976. Experimental subjects—who should they be? JAMA 235:2197.
9. May, W. E. 1974. Experimenting on human subjects. Linacre Q. 41:238–252.
10. Bartholome, W. G. 1976. The ethics of nontherapeutic clinical research on children. Proceedings of the National Commission for the Protection of Human Subjects of Biomedical and Behavioral Research. Hastings Cent. Rep. 6:44–45.

LAZARUS REVISITED
Moral and Spiritual Aspects of Experimental Therapeutics with Children

Kenneth Vaux

Sickness transforms life into a pilgrimage. When things are well and whole, we forget that life is a story. It seems to be static, constant, eternal. It seems to be parmenidean, to consist of recurrent patterns, developmental sequences, cycles, coming and going, then coming again. Awake at 6:30, to school at 7:30, dinner at 6, to sleep at 8:30. Yesterday and tomorrow; forever the same. Upward and downward trajectories, recurrent rhythms, stages of childhood, stages of decline, pre- and post-death stages; all the same, consistent, universal.

In life's illusion we are obsessively Greek; then comes sickness, and we are pilgrims once again. Life is a drama, not the Greek analogy but the Semitic story, not recapitulating themes but once and for all, forever unique, unrepeatable persons on an adventure. Life is an epic of judgment and grace. It is understandable only within the dimension of spirit.

The patient is a pilgrim, the physician, a defender-companion. The unknown must be explored. One must go to meet the dark night. One strains to see dawn break as darkness somehow softens.

John Donne was 50 years old when King James appointed him Dean of St. Paul's Cathedral in 1621. Shortly thereafter he became seriously ill and developed pneumonia. After several days of precipitous danger from both the disease and the treatments, he was lifted from his deathbed into health. Donne imposed on this experience the leitmotifs of his thought: 1) estrangement and lethal sickness, 2) the Messiah as healer, without whom the physician is impotent, and 3) the raising of Lazarus. His *Devotions* chronicle the spiritual pilgrimage of fear and reckoning, abandonment and rescue, exhaustion and ecstasy, that frame the experience of life-threatening illness. The outline of the *Devotions* shows the signposts of those traveling pilgrims, patient and physician:

The First Grudging of the Sickness
The Patient Takes His Bed
The Physician Comes
The Physician Is Afraid
The Disease Steals on Insensibly
They Use Cordials to Keep the Disease from the Heart
They Apply Pigeons to Draw the Vapours from the Head
The Sickness Declares Its Malignity by Spots
I Sleep Not Day or Night
The Bell Tolls for Another Telling Me I Must Die
At Last the Physician Sees Land
God Prospers Their Practice and by Them He Calls Me, Lazarus, Out
    of My Bed.

Dr. William Easson has coined a new phrase for the medical literature, "the Lazarus syndrome" (*1, 2*). Here the reality of lifethreatening disease overwhelms patient, physician, and family, and the hope for revivification is given up. Grief is done, separation occurs, the sick child is abandoned to fate, then unexpectedly is lifted out of the grave, a stranger. Reintegration into home, family, school, community becomes hard.

Easson's work and the wisdom of John Donne, particularly their use of the symbol of Lazarus, point us to the moral dialectics of experimentation and submission, hope and acceptance, that shape clinical research on children.

As we address the issue of experimental therapeutics with children, value considerations, meaning, and morals are the focus. I define experimental therapeutics as novel, unprecedented treatments that may or may not benefit the person involved or others in the future. I speak of treatments for children with life threatening illness, treatments that carry considerable chance of benefit and considerable risk. Although great ethical challenges remain in the problems of nontherapeutic research (such as research on an aborted viable fetus) and noninvasive research (such as analysis of leftover blood and urine samples), I feel the most ethically consequential research today is found in experimental therapeutics. This is particularly so in children because they provide what students of ethics have called the Grenzsituation, the borderline question. Here at the borders of both scientific and moral tradition, we probe questions that, when insight comes, bring clarity at the fundamental level and are generally applicable.

I speak from a defined clinical experience. For 10 years I have served on committees for human protection in Houston hospitals. For the last several years I have been a member of the pediatrics team at M. D. Anderson.

It may be helpful, by way of introduction, to recall the root values behind the activities of biomedical research on the one hand and biomedical ethics on the other. Both activities are born in the human impulse to serve other humans. Like all human endeavors, especially benevolence, these activities are often morally tainted by mixed motives. Biomedical research at root is prompted by our personal and collective desire to serve the well-being of our fellows. Of cardinal importance are the values of health and survival. Pursuit of these values is rooted in the passion to alleviate suffering. Like the Great Physician, we seek to rescue Lazarus from the jaws of death. In addition to these primary values, we find secondary values, such as the pursuit of knowledge and personal ambition. These primary and secondary values operate at the heart of that commitment of human energy and public resource we call biomedical research. We wish to know in order to save.

What about biomedical ethics? Here, the root impulse, if I may use Erik Erikson's phrase, is atonement as opposed to carnival. Carnival is that quality of personal and cultural animus engaging mind, heart, and will that generates creativity, science, experimentation, the venture into the unknown. Atonement is the other pole in the dialectic. Here we shrink back in hesitancy, remorse, and withdrawal from our excursions into the unknown. Here we seek to protect and conserve value already possessed. Eric Kahler has described the sixth-century Germanic warriors who ravaged the outposts of the Roman Empire, then sat down and wept in remorse at their conquest. The modern spirit of biomedical ethics is born in the atoning reaction to science cut loose from personal and even human value. Ours is the legacy of Nuremberg. From personal codes to institutional policies to national and international guidelines, biomedical ethics seeks to anchor, articulate, and activate these atoning values. These include such values as being informed, being left alone, being protected from and compensated for injury.

The human enterprise of medicine oscillates between the imperatives to "heal the sick" (carnival) and to "do no harm" (atonement), or, as Dr. Ramsey reminds us, "to do good and do no evil." Science lives for the betterment of man, law for the preservation of man. At certain moments, like the present, a strange inversion occurs. Science comes to conserve the human and personal, ethics come to serve the abstract good. Theologically speaking, this is a time when law overwhelms grace, caution tempers conquest. Some would say that in this day of defensive medicine and aggressive law, we actually harm persons in the name of protecting them.

Sick children come to our department at M. D. Anderson because they believe the innovative to be the best treatment or because all other treatments have failed. Driven by desperation and amazing hope, they show up at Anderson as they do at Roswell Park, Sloan-Kettering, and the Mayo Clinic. They meet a team of eight senior physicians, associates, fellows, residents, interns; an entourage of some of the finest scientist-clinicians in the world. The work of the department is organized around dozens of research protocols. They are placed in Phase III, II, and I studies; from the tried and tested to the novel and risk-fraught. The protocols apply to patients with diseases grouped under hematology, solid tumor, histiocytosis, brain tumor, leukemia, and lymphoma. After diagnosis and lab work, the patient is given the option of no treatment, standard treatment, or research investigation. In some cases those electing the traditional treatment become the control arm for the research group. In the new protocols some are assigned to the test arm, some to the control arm. The computer often designates which patients receive which program. With some patients, historical and experiential controls are used. This means that the physician judges where the individual patient is in terms of his or her disease, and bases the treatment on intuition formed by previous experience.

What are the problems? Randomization is a profound ethical question. The research clinician must simultaneously hold three opinions:

1. The experimental treatment is best. That the clinician conceived, developed, and defended the grant proposal indicates this belief. The grant would not be approved if there were not substantial evidence to support it.

2. The question is still open; A may be as good as B. The clinician must hold this open opinion to ethically condone putting some people in the control arm.
3. The new treatment may be worse than the accepted, perhaps even worse than nothing at all. This is more often true with studies involving patients who have gone through several protocols and with Phase II and I studies.

Lively debate goes on as to whether our customary experimental research design—with its controls, double blinds, placebos, and statistical verification—is intrinsically unethical. Randomization remains a necessity, required by good science and the carneval values, but it is becoming more difficult to justify it on an ethical basis. We must improve patient advocacy and compensation measures.

As we survey the moral topography, we confront informed consent, a central theme of our conference. The movement for informed consent accomplished much good, given the demand of some scientists, including physicians, to be unhindered. However, to think that fully informed consent is possible is a dangerous illusion. Beecher put it succinctly: "Informed consent is not there for the asking." We need to explore what Inglefinger calls "educated consent." With children, the great problem of proxy or vicarious consent emerges. Fortunately, we have recently discovered the amazing capacity of children even 4 years old to participate, with some knowledgability, in the processes of informing and consenting.

The law sometimes results in overkill. Consider the following consent form chosen at random from our protocols.

> Parents and patients will be told all the known side effects of Velban and bleomycin. These will include granulocytopenia, thrombocytopenia, anemia, nausea, vomiting, anorexia, stomatitis, weight loss, constipation or diarrhea, loss of deep tendon reflexes, paresthesia, peripheral neuropathy, constipation, hoarseness, ptosis, double vision, alopecia, fever, chills, skin rash, hypotension, pruritis, cough, dyspnea, anaphylaxis, and pulmonary fibrosis. In addition to all above, there may be some unknown side effects of each drug. Combination of these drugs may cause some immunosuppression resulting in unpredicted serious or fatal infections.

The diffculties are evident. The doctors I work with are extremely careful at this point. They know that patients are caught up in a desperate yearning for restoration of health, with mingled hope and delusion, honesty and fantasy. Physicians share the natural human propensity to deny the tragic and heighten the hopeful. They do not want to fail, although ultimately they always must. Often the patient or family will ask the physician, "If I were your child, what would you do?" The physician who is invited to engage the patient at a deeply human level should not evade the opportunity. A noted Mayo clinic physician once told a small group of medical people, "If they open me up and cancer is spread, don't do anything. Close me up. Keep me comfortable and let me go. But I could never raise this option with a patient." The time-honored tradition among researchers of putting themselves in the experimental situation either literally or empathetically is a rich ethical response to the golden rule. It should be nurtured in personal and public policy.

Any analysis of the context of experimental therapeutics must consider the high drama of this environment. On wards in which children are critically ill, deep emotions—fear, guilt, rage, hope, love—oscillate wildly. "Are we doing everything possible?" "What about this new medicine in Mexico?" "Maybe we should try Laetrile." "Kathryn Kuhlman is in town, should we go?" People stumble along a rocky road, driven blindly; time is foreshortened, pain and reprieve, diminishing returns, vanishing changes, myelosuppression.

Dramatic breakthroughs sometimes occur, as in leukemia, Wilms' tumor, and Hodgkin's disease. Today "the Lazarus syndrome" occurs more frequently. Back from the brink of death, new problems present themselves. The child may be cured, but we are not prepared for that. We had better well know what we are doing when we rescue persons from the grave. We must insure that restoration accompanies rescue. Two of our "truly cured" patients are now on trial for murder; this raises the question of the wholeness of their "cure."

Think of the distancing games that patients, parents, and physicians play. Games patients play: "The doctor is too busy to be disturbed by this question," "I should know what dyspoopsia is and what a groinocologist does; I would seem as ignorant as Archie Bunker if I asked," "I am brave; I cannot let anyone know I am scared." Games physicians play: "I'm very busy, am I not?" "I cannot say anything that will let the patient think I am discouraged," "I could not possibly suggest no treatment as one of the alternative approaches." Games parents play: "Obey Mother and Father and everyone bigger than you," "Good kids take their medicine," "We cannot let her know how scared we are."

The tension between research and ethics, carnival and atonement, must be maintained for there to be a therapeutic community. Let me finally advocate some guidelines that will aid in morally resolving these agonizing questions.

Absolute honesty is essential. Sickness in children should not be compounded by deception, deviousness, and denial. We have all seen the bitter aftermath of evasions and lies. We have also seen the courage and comfort that develop when truth is honored. Federal guidelines, hospital educational programs, and training modules for doctors and nurses should all safeguard this virtue.

Regarding informed consent, we must be very careful to honor the human freedom both to consent and to refrain from consenting. The policy of rendering children "therapeutic orphans" by refusing them the opportunity to participate in research needs to be reexamined. Hypercaution in the name of human protection can limit potential health benefits. Even in nonbeneficial research, children should have the option to exercise their native altruism.

Given our frightened and frantic mania to "do something, anything," the dangerous convergence of "ravenous consumers and rapacious providers" (Ivan Illich), the absurd tendency to stumble along thoughtlessly until death intervenes on the floor of the ICU surrounded by broken vials, tubes, and resuscitation machines; given all these, we must reaffirm the ancient ars moriendi, artful suffering and death, against the vitalistic manias of medicine. The new Massachusetts General guidelines for hopelessly ill patients, the hospice movement, the growing willingness to go home and begin the painkiller known as Brompton's mixture, are signals of this emerging wisdom.

Finally, we must nurture humility in all who minister amid these traumas. This virtue is necessary for good science and humane therapeutics. It is only when one learns to contemplate nature (betrachten), said Kepler, that one can understand nature. When dealing with man, that profound reach of nature, this is particularly true. Humility, earthiness (humus), humor; it is all the same. The essence of humility is setting aside self-obsession in favor of concern for others.

Many modern writers have reflected on the moral meaning of Lazarus, including Eugene O'Neill (*Lazarus Laughed*) and Sylvia Plath ("Lady Lazarus"). C. S. Lewis reflects on the death by cancer of his beloved wife, Joy, in *A Grief Observed:*

> What sort of a lover am I to think so much about my affliction and so much less about hers? Even the insane call "come back" is all for my

own sake. I never even raised the question whether such a return, if it were possible, would be good for her. I want her back as an ingredient in the restoration of my past. Could I have wished her anything worse? Having got once through death, to come back and then, at some later date, have all her dying to do over again? They call Stephen the first martyr. Hadn't Lazarus a rawer deal? (3).

We began with words of the English cleric John Donne. Another English canon, who had often witnessed the anguish of life at the brink, the consumptive heat of pneumonia, wrote:

Lord support us all the day long
until the shadows lengthen
and the busy world is hushed
and the fever of life is over
and our work is done—
Then in thy mercy, grant us a safe lodging,
an eternal rest—and peace at the last (4).

REFERENCES

1. Easson, W. M. 1972. The Lazarus syndrome in childhood. Medical Insight 4:47.
2. Easson, W. M. 1970. The Dying Child. Charles C. Thomas, Springfield, Ill.
3. Lewis, C. S. 1960. A Grief Observed. Beacon Press, Boston.
4. Newman, J. H. The Book of Common Prayer.

DISCUSSING THE ETHICS OF RESEARCH ON CHILDREN

Jerome Berryman

We adults talk a lot about children. Our discussions usually stereotype what children think and feel, because they are not present to challenge our false assumptions, directly with words or indirectly by their actions. Our adult conversation about children in this workshop is not untypical. We have present physicians, scientists, ethicists, lawyers, educators, and theologians, but we need some children to speak for themselves.

We adults all speak partial truths about children becoming subjects of research. The ethicists and lawyers tend to assume that they ought to decide what children can and should think and feel. They speak of "voiceless children," "the not comprehending child," "the unperceiving child," and "the child incapable of making his or her own choices." It is true that children do not think and feel as adults do, but the conclusion that they should not be included in the ethical discussion is a cruel distortion of what I consider to be the main purpose of having an ethical discussion with another human being, especially with a child. The main point is to be with children on the threshold of unknown territory and to let them know that you will stay with them through their sickness and the proposed research. The right involved is the right not to be abandoned by another of one's species, and the correlated duty is the duty to be a translator across the developmental distance between the adult and the child, rather than to acquiesce to it.

John Holt represents the position of a perceptive educator and child advocate. He urges on us another partial truth. Saying that we cannot know anyone in his or her depths, regardless of age or stage of development, is only partially true, because the answer to overgeneralization is not overparticularization. The cure for both distortions is to be so fluent in your general knowledge of children that you can freely depart from it in the presence of an individual child when it is dictated (and it always is). Cramming people into developmental molds only means that the person doing the stuffing is rigidly projecting his or her uninformed, general knowledge. However, using knowledge of developmental trends as a reference point can help prevent one from projecting unexamined assumptions about an individual child.

The physicians and scientists speak partial truths in terms of what can be counted, weighed, measured, and reduced to numbers about cancer. The implication is that the child is a cancer container and that cancer is their real point of interest. Although narrowing one's focus into an area of specialization leads to advances in research, the truth is partial because the child and the cancer cannot be separated. The war on cancer is also a war for healthy, developing, happy children. The scientists and physicians at M. D. Anderson have this as their goal, and this conference is a struggle to keep the children in focus, but the fact remains that the truth they speak is only partial.

The partial truth I want to put forward is that the primary purpose of having an ethical discussion with children or adults is to unlock their loneliness. To talk about what another person ought to do with them is to come close to that place of unspeakable dreads and hopes, for centuries recognized by children in fairy tales that start at the edge of a dark and dangerous forest. How will they find their way and who will be their guide?

The ethical conversation ought to be an end in itself, an antidote to deep loneliness. It is not a debate or combat. It is a sign of the love and caring that only members of the same species can give each other. This is true whether we seek to enable the child to consent to research and make an informed decision about it or to obtain the child's assent to a course of action that parents, friends, relatives, or doctors have already decided on. How much the child should be the decision-maker depends on how each family and child make decisions and how well the adults hear and speak the child's language.

I wish to say a few words about why we adults tend to not recognize our duty to be with children in their loneliness and to become good translators. I would then like to outline how I see the entire ethical process so we can concentrate on the structuralist aspect of that process. We can then focus on the structural differences between the thinking of adults and that of children and try to find a way to neutralize the developmental distance between us with special reference to three questions that the child has but does not always express: "What are you going to do to me?" "Why must I do it [the research]?" "What if it doesn't work?" I intend to suggest ways in which the adult and the child can be together despite their developmental structural differences. If these ways can carry such a burden, then we can "live happily ever after" with the child, despite the dangers in the dark forest of research and threatened health.

In earlier times children were so invisible that the concept of "childhood" did not exist. There were infants and there were adults. The real distinction was made when infants were no longer dependent on their mothers or nurses for their physical needs (*1*).

Despite a tremendous gain in adults' ability to conceive of and to know children, we still seem to operate generally by two myopic myths. We continue to think that children will understand if we talk to them as if they are adults, and we think that they are always happy, or at least they ought to be so. Our myopia is probably rooted in not wanting to see the world of the child because there are parts we would not like to remember and because of the obligations to be a trustworthy guide it would place on us. There is also the fact anyone knows who has lived in a foreign country. It takes a great deal of patience, energy, and good will, as well as skill, to be a good translator.

Carole Klein has written with sensitivity, respect, and informed insight of the emotional world of the child. In *How It Feels to Be a Child* (*2*), she carefully removes the mask with the painted smile on it to examine the child's fears, loneliness, guilt, anger, dreams, shame, sexual feelings, and emotions mixed up with parents and parenting persons. We will now turn to the child's thinking as we discuss the ethical domain, but the feelings are of equal importance.

THE ETHICAL DOMAIN: AN ECLECTIC VIEW

When one thinks of moral reasoning and ethics, there is a tendency to think only in terms of decision making or the structures of moral reasoning. There is a wider domain for our ethical discussion with the child that includes perception of the facts, reasoning about them, the faith context in which one decides and acts, and evaluation of one's action. This is a closed process that begins again with either the same or a new perception of the world of facts, depending on the results of the evaluation. It takes several research traditions to trace the structures and content of the process through this fact, reasoning, acting, and evaluation system.

The first part of the process deals with the "facts." What we see as facts involves our needs. Need levels have been studied by Maslow (*3*). We tend to see what we need to see. The structures by which we think about the world of facts have been studied by Piaget (*4*). His work adds an appreciation for the mental structures in the developing concept of causality by which the facts are tied together.

In the judgment phase of the ethics process, one must rank one's values to decide what to do. Rokeach has studied this process (*5*), which provides the content for the judgment along with the facts. This content is woven together with thought structures used in moral reasoning. These structures have been isolated into six developmental stages by Kohlberg (*6*). He has suggested that the higher the development, the more likely one is to do what one thinks one ought to do. At the highest stage, however, one encounters the cosmic perspective and asks, "Why be moral?" Kohlberg's analysis spills over into questions of faith and religion in his discussion of despair.

The content of the third phase of the ethics process is the developing ego strengths that have been traced by Erikson (*7*) through eight stages of psychosocial crises. The faith climate has been studied structurally by Fowler (*8*), who has isolated six "faithing" structures that include the work of Piaget in logic and Kohlberg in moral reasoning. If one does not have a clear sense of one's faith world, a "trustable" environment, then the paralysis of anxiety very likely sets in. One senses a danger, but cannot identify it. One does not know whether to stand and fight or flee. Decision and action are paralyzed. The structures of faith and the content of one's ego strength are both interwoven with the judgment and acting aspects of this ethics process. They also look forward to the evaluation that follows.

The evaluation part of the ethics process expands on the "operant conditioning" analysis of B. F. Skinner, going beyond his hesitation to explore beneath the skin for meaning to include motivation as well as reinforcement issues. As we monitor our reinforcement, we continually adjust in ways that are not always clear to us, but there are occasions when we do struggle to make something new. The "something new" might be in terms of content, such as new ideas or visions of the world, or in terms of new structures by which to assimilate the world and be in equilibrium with its structures.

There are times when we are not satisfied with the status quo, even when it is positively reinforcing. At other times the environment reinforces us negatively and yet there is the inner motivation to overcome that pain to find something new. This is true in individual cases, although not significant statistically.

The one kind of evaluation calls for something new in terms of content. In the tension of the painful old and the anticipated new, random thoughts begin to break to the surface of consciousness, often in art or in dreams. This is the primary process kind of thinking discussed by Freud and expanded on by Maslow (*10*) and later by Arieti (*11*). These random ideas are an amorphous cognition that is consciously and analytically worked through by the secondary process, which tests it against the present view of reality. The synthesis of the old and new realities creates the new world of "facts" in which ethical situations are seen.

The second kind of evaluation deals not with the content of new ideas, but with the structures for thinking about reality. A structural disequilibrium gives rise to the motivation to reestablish balance. The structures of the mind change to better match the structures in the outside world whether in nature, such as causality, or in society, as with moral reasoning, or in the ultimate environment, with faith.

This account of evaluation as a kind of creativity completes the circuit of the ethical process. The feelings have been carried by what we have called the "content" aspect of the circuit and the relations between these feelings have been carried in the form of what we have called "structures." Our goal now is to see how these structures can block or aid communication between the adult and the child as together they deal with the emotionally charged ethical questions surrounding proposed research in which the child is the subject.

INTERSTAGE COMMUNICATION: A KEY

The structures we have been discussing fall into stages. Our discussion with the child about how the research works involves the stages of thinking about causality that Piaget isolated. To discuss the question of whether the child ought to become a subject for research involves us in the use of the stages isolated by Kohlberg for doing moral reasoning. To discuss what there is to ultimately rely on and trust, we need to use the structures isolated by Fowler by which we do our "faithing." All three of these persons hold the following assumptions about the way these stages work:

1. Stages are action systems.
2. Transformation of structures from stage to stage cannot be explained by associationist learning (contiguity, repetition, reinforcement, etc.), but only by the development of organizational wholes or systems of internal relations.
3. The development of cognitive structures is the result of the interaction between the structure of the organism and the structure of the environment, rather than the direct result of maturation or of learning in the sense of shaping the organism's responses to accord with environmental structures.
4. The direction of the development of the structure is toward greater equilibrium in the organism-environmental interaction so that the individual neither is dominated by the perceived object or situation nor dominates it, but allows for balanced interaction.
5. The stage development process is hierarchical and invariant. One does not get to stage 4 before going through stages 1, 2, and 3. One does not lose the ability to use the earlier stages.
6. Although the content can vary as to thoughts and feelings that accompany thoughts, the structures are uniform. Both Piaget and Kohlberg have had their stage theories verified across cultural lines.

The key to talking between these structures is to understand what kind of communication can take place between different stages. Rest, Turiel, and Kohlberg studied this question to discover the appropriate way to intervene to promote moral development. Their study was reviewed by Rest in 1973 and again commented on in 1976 (*12–14*). Two things are relevant to our interests: stage comprehension and stage preference.

Stage comprehension was first determined by asking the subjects about moral dilemmas and scoring the structures in their discussions of what was fair in each situation. The subjects were then given samples of six different stages of response and asked to rephrase them in their own words. The recasting of these stages in their own words was then compared to the subjects' spontaneous stages. It was discovered that the restatements of the stage that was one above a subject's spontaneous stage tended to be cast in the logic of the spontaneous stage. This tendency grew more pronounced the farther from one's spontaneous stage the statements moved.

Stage preference was studed in addition to stage comprehension. Among three alternatives for preference $(-1, +1, +2)$, the stage least preferred was one stage below one's spontaneous stage. The second most often rejected was two stages above one's customary stage of thinking. The most preferred of the three alternatives was one stage above one's most used stage.

Since we are looking for optimum communication, we should aim first for a match with the child's spontaneous stage. If we are in doubt, we might aim a bit high as a second choice, because there would still be good comprehension one stage above the spontaneous stage and the child's preference is the greatest for this stage. If we try to communicate at a stage below, it will be rejected as too naive, and if we try to communicate two stages above, it will probably be garbled in the child's translation into his or her spontaneous stage.

Missing the mark can have tragic results. In the first place, the children will not really be informed about the facts of the research in a way they understand. This not only infringes on their right to be informed, but also prevents them from knowing how to help in the research and healing process. Second, the children will be out of touch with the adults around them. Third, they will not only feel the distance between them and adults, but will begin to wonder if their own perception of reality is wrong because adults say it is. They will begin to mistrust their own perceptions in this process that Laing has called "the policies of experience" (15), when self-estrangement is the last thing they need.

With this discussion of interstage communication in mind, we can turn to the three specific areas in which we might expect to discuss the proposed research with the child. These will correspond roughly to the first three parts discussed in the ethics process.

WHAT ARE YOU GOING TO DO TO ME?

The first question concerns the natural reality in the research. It is a question about science, but we must refer to Piaget's research into the child's concept of causality to know better how to answer the question in his or her terms. Piaget's fourth book, *The Child's Conception of Physical Causality,* written with the help of 17 collaborators, is our source (4).

The researchers used several approaches. They asked the children to tell them how things such as clouds and water moved. Another approach was half verbal and half experiential. They enumerated movements and parts of machines and asked why and how the movements were performed. A purely experiential approach used simple experiments, such as dropping a pebble in a glass of water. The children were asked how and why the pebble went down. Children were also asked to draw pictures of bicycles to show how the parts worked together.

Seventeen kinds of causality were isolated; these fell into rough stages from birth to 2 years, 2 to 7, 7 to 12, and over 12. Table 1 shows the types seen at the stage from 2 to 7 and 7 to 12 years.

The listing of the types of causality distinguished by Piaget and his colleagues suggests the carefulness with which adults need to listen to children to learn how they see the world of nature. This same care-

Table 1.   Types of causality as distinguished by Piaget

Age 2 to 7—precausality	
1. Motivational	Things and events are sent by God or people
2. Finalistic	The last step defines the reason
3. Phenomenistic	Simultaneous events are causally linked
4. Participatory	Similar things are related causally
5. Magical	Acts, gestures, or words cause events or protect from events
6. Moral	A theory or event exists because it is necessary
7. Artificialistic	Someone turns on events
8. Animistic	Internal forces, alive and conscious, shape things
9. Dynamic	Physical internal forces cause movement
Age 7 to 12—true causality	
1. Reaction to surrounding medium	The surrounding medium supplies continued force impetus
2. Mechanical	Outside forces cause movement
3. Generation	One event or thing is the mother of another
4. Substantial identification	No more birth and growth of things, but some idea of mass needed to have one thing generate another
5. Condensation and rarefaction	Matter differs by degree of packing
6. Atomistic	Ultimate matter is conceived
7. Spatial	Use of perspective is employed in cause and effect
8. Logical deduction	Density and specific gravity are becoming concepts on causality

ful listening is needed to match one's discussion of the research with the level of causality understanding of the child.

Although we will concentrate, in the three questions children have in mind about research, on the ages from 2 to 7 and 7 to 12, it may be helpful to mention what comes before and after the two stages of causal conception identified above. From birth to 2 years, the child's view of the world is self-centric and is locked in a sensorimotor record for the most part, rather than in language. When children turn the instrument of physical action onto themselves for discovery, as previously they used it on the world about them, they discover an inner consciousness, a self. This self then becomes the index for understanding everything else in the world. Everything has a living, conscious center of causation within it, as the self does. The child becomes a naive theologian and sees spirits in everything.

Three general kinds of development carry the child forward from birth through 7 years. The first evolution is desubjectification. The tendency to see the world entirely in personal terms gradually fades. Second, the ability to trace a series in time develops. The feeling of "before and after" develops, along with differentiation of time and space, until the child can fill in the intermediary steps between cause and effect. A third line of evolution is the progressing ability to form and break down classes and see equivalences in different shapes. The child develops the ability to rearrange mentally what he or she could rearrange physically. The first and third strands of development have general application, whereas the second one, causal links, is unique to the development of the child's concept of causation. These evolutions finally stabilize into a new set of relationships to form the stage of causality conception outlined in Piaget's phrase "true causality."

During the period from 7 to 12 years, the gains along these three lines of development continue and consolidate. Children move from a world they interpret as naive theologians to a world they interpret as naive empiricists. They slowly develop desubjectification, the sense of before and after, and the ability to handle classes and equivalences, until their fascination with facts begins to fade and they move, about age 12, into the world as discovered by the new naive logician. Their confidence moves from what they can hold in their hands or perceive through their other senses to what they can develop by logical necessity. They move, in Piaget's terms, from transduction to induction and finally to deduction.

How, then, shall we answer the naive theologians or the naive empiricists when they ask what will happen to them in the research proposed? We need more than words alone. Children throughout these two periods need something to work with to really understand what is going to happen. A rag doll works very nicely.

The way one holds a doll tells a child a lot. You can show the child what is going to happen without going into details. The doll can be left with the child to accompany him or her in the research and the nurse can carry out her duties with the doll first so the child will know what is going to happen. Questions can be posed to the doll that the child might not be willing to discuss directly.

The naive theologians will understand what they are talking about if everything is personalized. The fluids "want" to come and make the child better. Even chemotherapy or surgery can be personalized this way. There are many animistic or theological nuances throughout the hospital that we adults have lost the ability to see. The naive theologians may be the most difficult to translate for because we adults often learned painfully that we were stupid and silly when we thought like that. It is hard to get over approaching the world as filled with "thou's" and the intimation of a larger "Thou." That kind of thinking is weeded out by parents and stamped out in school, but with it goes a whole kind of knowledge that is difficult to apprehend in any other way.

The naive empiricists still connect the why with the how, so they have moral questions at the outer limits of their causal conceptions. They want to know how it is really going to work, but they don't want you to overanswer. The doll will be as useful for them as for the naive theologians, but they will talk to and be with the doll in a slightly different way. Playing out the research procedure will be very helpful for both the naive theologians and the naive empiricists, but the latter will need more help getting everything together because they will be interested in more details in their play.

The doll is, finally, a multistage medium through which much of the translating can take place without having to have a perfect match of structures. Not only do children need to have concrete objects to move around to do their "thinking," but showing eases some of the burden on the logic structures for communicating. Moreover, the doll is an intermediary between the two parties to the conversation. It introduces a primitive "objectivity" to the meeting that would not be present if the adult used the child to show what was going to happen. This reduces some of the emotional charge to the conversation.

The doll is not a perfect example of what I mean by a "multistage medium" for communication. The parables used in the next two sections are, because the adult and the child participate in the same medium with the same words, although their understanding of the meaning in the medium can be very different. More conscious translating by the adult is required for the use of the doll than is required in the parables, when presented correctly. With this in mind, we can turn to the next aspect of the ethical discussion with the child.

WHY MUST I DO IT?

The previous question raised issues infused with moral considerations for the child from 2 to 7 to 12 years of age. We move now from a discussion of the facts in the moral situation (good ethics require good facts) to moral reasoning about the situation, from questions of natural reality to social reality questions. As we have implied already, in the young child these two questions are not very differentiated, but for purposes of analysis we have separated them here.

The developmental structuralist approach to this question probably began with Socrates as recorded by Plato, but the work of Kohlberg in recent years has been the most helpful.

Kohlberg builds on Piaget's research tradition and findings, despite the fact that he sometimes refers to his findings as "warmed-over Dewey." Piaget's stages of logical structures are considered necessary but not sufficient for stage changes in moral reasoning. This is because the logic stage may have been developed through interaction with the natural world, but not yet faced with structures in the social world that cause the imbalance motivating accommodation and stage development.

Moral reasoning is divided roughly into three large periods: preconventional, conventional, and postconventional thinking. Most Americans fall into the range of stages 3 and 4 by the time they are adults. They employ conventional moral reasoning. The children we are considering, those from 2 to 7 and 7 to 12 years of age, typically engage in preconventional moral thinking. A summary of Kohlberg's stages is important so we can better grasp some of the problems involved in interstage communication (Table 2).

The relevance of these stages is apparent at once. Talking with children about how it is fair for them to be research subjects in terms of universal principles or a social contract would be heard in garbled bits and pieces as premoral or preconventional reasoning. The strain of trying to understand that sort of talk would soon turn off the attempt to listen and children would begin to give adult-pleasing

Table 2.   Stages in moral reasoning (Kohlberg)

Premoral reasoning (2–7 years)	
Stage 0	No moral reasoning present.
Preconventional moral reasoning (7–12 years)	
Stage 1	Punishment and reward in physical terms.
Stage 2	Trade-off as yardstick of fairness.
Conventional moral reasoning (12+ years)	
Stage 3	Good behavior as measured against peer and social groups.
Stage 4	Legal measures of justice and fairness.
Postconventional reasoning (12+ years)	
Stage 5	Laws can be changed to meet needs (social utilitarianism).
Stage 6	Social reference extends to all humankind.
Stage 7	Cosmic perspective—overt philosophy and religion.

answers to bring the discomfort to an end. Loneliness would remain locked.

A discussion employing conventional reasoning would be better heard. The duty of the children in terms of sacred or political law, however, would probably still be heard in terms of adults laying down the law with implications of physical reward and punishment. Stage 3 type reasoning involving feelings of the family or classmates or some other special group might be heard for what the adult was saying. For example, it might make sense to become a research subject to help another person if that person were in a relevant group and known by the child.

The moral imperative to try to match the child's structural stage remains so that the discussion can become an end in itself, the end being to be with the child in a profound way. The difficulty of making that perfect match is obvious. The adult cannot employ his or her own moral reasoning. Translation of structures changes one's moral position, although the outcomes, the "Yes" or "No," might remain the same. This puts the adult under a strain that might block out the message. Perhaps using a multistage medium to share the discussion can help. This is not to say that one should not try for a perfect match in structures, but only that this multistage medium might hedge one's bet a bit and also be a better way to be with the child than reliance on language alone.

One multistage medium I have been experimenting with has been the parables of Jesus of Nazareth. They seem able to provide fruitful interaction with any stage of reasoning. This ambiguity makes them an ideal mode of communication for two persons at different stages of reasoning. Each can remain true to his or her way of expressing the moral question and yet be in deep communion with the other person. This means that the nonverbal communication will not flood the child with mixed signals.

The Parable of the Good Samaritan is a good example. It should be presented with an economy of words and with concrete materials for its multistage nature to really work. I use golden boxes as settings for the parables and have one that shows how a parable is a story inside a story like a box can be inside a box. All the props are laid out on an underlay, which in this case is burlap to represent the desert. Other props include a strip of felt for the road, a city at either end, and black felt rocks on the side of the road. The figures include the person who was hurt and left beside the road, as well as the two persons who "passed by on the other side" and the Samaritan who stopped to help. They are two-dimensional and laminated to slide over the underlay and felt as the story is told.

After the presentation of the parable, the child and the adult can wonder together who was really a "neighbor" or friend to the person who was hurt. The child can pick from among the figures who he or she would like to be. The discussion can be extended by paintings of the parable, and the parable box can be left with the child so he can work it through again alone.

Even if children grasp the facts of the situation, work through their ethical position with a parable, and want to help themselves or another person by being research subjects, the ethical discussion is not complete. They also need discussion of certain faith questions with facts and moral reasoning, to establish both the trust to go forward and something to rely on if things do not happen as planned. That question is discussed next.

WHAT IF IT DOES NOT WORK OUT?

This question moves us beyond both natural and social reality to ultimate reality. It is more than a question about the child's death if the research does not succeed. It is a question of what the child or anyone can rely on when, despite one's understanding of science and one's best moral judgment, things do not work out. It has to do with how one's whole world hangs together.

The structures of faith development have been studied by James Fowler (9). The structuralist and visceral approaches seem complementary. Both are necessary to adequately grasp the faith phenomenon. We will limit our discussion here, however, to the contribution of the structuralists to discussing ethical questions with children in their fullest form.

Building on the research and method of Piaget and Kohlberg, Fowler identified six stages of faith development. Each stage is averaged by scoring persons on seven variables within each stage. The variables used to determine one's faith stage average are: the structures of logic, world coherence, role-taking, authority, bounds of social awareness, form of moral judgment, and the role of symbols. The structures of faith development extend beyond the interaction with the natural world examined by Piaget and interaction with the social world examined by Kohlberg to the interaction with the most comprehensive limits to one's life. Faith stages include logic and moral reasoning stages. Logic is necessary but not sufficient for a faith stage change (Table 3).

As a medium for multistage communication about ultimate reality, I would like to suggest the Parable of the Good Shepherd. Part of my work at the Institute of Religion has been to examine many media to see if they have this capacity. Certainly sacraments do. Probably sacred history and sacred ethics do if they are presented carefully and appropriately. Prayer and liturgy probably do, too, when presented appropriately. This is something that religions have known by intuition for centuries, but must continually be rediscovered.

Table 3.   Stages in faith development (Fowler)

Stage 1	Episodic and alogical world view.
Stage 2	Mythical-literal world view; authority relates to trust; limited social awareness (around age 6).
State 3	Ideas shape world view; tradition is recognized; symbolism is multidimensional (around age 12).
Stage 4	Ultimate matters are either/or questions.
Stage 5	Rarely achieved. Dialectical logic is typical; universal moral principles (around age 30).
Stage 6	Very rarely achieved. Transcendent loyalty, ontological awareness (around age 40).

I am indebted to Professoressa Sofia Cavalletti of Rome for having rediscovered much of how to use these multistage media with children in our time. Her entry point was made by applying the Montessori method to the teaching of religion to young children. Of all her insights, the use of the Parable of the Good Shepherd seems to be the most profound. This can also be presented using simple strips of cloth and figures.

Although the details of the presentation may differ, when children are asked to paint back the parables, the same sorts of paintings appear at different stages. Children from about 2 to 7 years paint the sheepfold with the sheep inside as the dominant feature. Beginning at about age 7, the Good Shepherd begins to dominate. By about age 12, the children become interested in the difference in "leadership" between the Good Shepherd and the Ordinary Shepherd. Regardless of what aspect of the parable the children focus on, they seldom confuse the Good Shepherd with their parents. He is something bigger and more comprehensive in his constant caring.

Like fairy tales, the parables of Jesus communicate on many different levels. One brings to them what one knows and the structures by which one knows. They are something to walk with through the journey of human faith. They do not contain the growth of someone beginning his or her journey and they retain many levels of meaning on which a person late in the journey can reflect. Often an unspoken need can guide a person to one parable or another. It certainly does for the children who cannot explain why they want to do a certain parable over and over again. Of all the parables, the one most important for children in a hospital seems to be that of the Good Shepherd.

There is a difference between parables and fairy tales that is also important for the child in the hospital discussing with an adult the prospects of research in which he or she will be the subject. Fairy tales are about the realities of growing up, but these children are faced with having their growing up cut short. Many of the parables are about an invisible kingdom within and among us that continues to grow despite all, even failing physical health. Parables such as the one about heaven or the mustard seed say this in ways that one is hard pressed to exhaust or improve on.

In any case, the use of such a multistage medium as the Parable of the Good Shepherd helps us communicate with the child across the developmental distance. Being in the parable with the child unlocks his or her loneliness and allows the adult to be a companion in the child's dangerous journey.

"LIVING HAPPILY EVER AFTER"

In striving to clarify what the developmental structuralists have to say about our ethical conversations with children, I have had a twofold hope. On the one hand, I wanted to widen the concept of the ethical discussion to include the whole ethical domain, the facts, the reasoning, and the "faithing." If we were going to deal with more than one ethical conversation, we would have gone further into the part evaluation and creativity play. My second hope was to provide some insight into how adults can become better translators in their conversations with children about matters of ultimate importance, such as whether or not a child ought to become a subject of research. Both hopes, the why and the how of the process, were formulated to help unlock the loneliness of the child faced with such a situation.

Bettelheim has noted that, when fairy tales end with the formula "and they lived happily ever after," the child does not fix on the promise of eternal life to take the sting out of dying and illness (*16*). They end that way to assure the child that a satisfying bond between human beings can form despite being lost or suffering trials in dark forests or in the land of the giants. The promise is there of emotional security and permanence, despite their flooding emotions. The parables go even farther. They say, in their many ways and on many levels, that everything is really a Thou, as the naive theologians of 2 to 7 years sense, and that the Thou loves them in a way that keeps on growing, despite everything.

REFERENCES

1. Aries, P. 1962. Centuries of Childhood (Robert Baldick, trans.). Vintage Books, New York.
2. Klein, C. 1975. How It Feels to Be a Child. Harper and Row, New York.
3. Maslow, A. H. 1954. Motivation and Personality. Harper and Row, New York.
4. Piaget, J. 1951. The Child's Conception of Physical Causality. Routledge & Kegan Paul Ltd., London.
5. Rokeach, M. 1973. The Nature of Human Values. The Free Press, New York.

6. Kohlberg, L. 1969. Stage and sequence: the cognitive-developmental approach to socialization. In: Handbook of Socialization Theory and Research. pp. 347–480. Rand McNally & Company, Chicago.

7. Kohlberg, L. 1973. Continuities in childhood and adult moral development revisited. In: Collected Papers on Moral Development and Moral Education. Center for Moral Education, Graduate School of Education, Harvard University, Cambridge, Mass.

8. Erikson, E. 1963. Childhood and Society. 2nd Ed. W. W. Norton & Company Inc., New York.

9. Berryman, J. (Ed.). 1977. Life Maps: The Journey of Human Faith. Wexford Press, Boston.

10. Maslow, A. 1971. The Farther Reaches of Human Nature. Viking Press, New York.

11. Arieti, S. 1976. Creativity: The Magic Synthesis. Basic Books, New York.

12. Rest, J., Turiel, E., and Kohlberg, L. 1969. Level of moral development as a determinant of preferences and comprehension of moral judgment made by others. J. Pers. 37:225–252.

13. Rest, J. 1973. The hierarchical nature of stages of moral judgment. J. Pers. 41:86–109.

14. Rest, J. 1977. The research base of the cognitive developmental approach to moral education. In: T. Hennessy (ed.), Values and Moral Development. Paulist Press, New York.

15. Laing, R. D. 1976. Politics of Experience. Ballantine Books, New York.

16. Bettelheim, B. 1976. The Uses of Enchantment. Alfred A. Knopf Inc., New York.

LEGAL AND SOCIETAL CONSTRAINTS

THE LEGAL DIMENSIONS OF RESEARCH ON CHILDREN
An Introduction

Leonard L. Riskin

For what purposes, under what conditions, and upon which children should this society permit biomedical research to be carried out? This is the question that inspired this conference. We struggle mightily with it because we are not agreed about the rights and responsibilities of parents and about the capacity or rights of children to intelligently agree to participate in research, because we assign different values to research, and because we attribute different meanings to such expressions as "risk-benefit" and "informed consent."

But resolve this issue we must. The primary organ for recommending a solution is the National Commission for the Protection of Subjects of Biomedical and Behavioral Research. Since November 1976, its staff has produced two sets of draft recommendations, the second of which is, at this writing, under consideration by the full commission. It is not hard to sympathize with the commission and with the HEW policy-makers who will receive its proposals. State courts and legislatures have given them almost no specific guidance, and ethical leaders seem hopelessly at loggerheads.

The commission's recommendations, if adopted by HEW in the form of regulations, will have enormous impact, applying to HEW-sponsored projects in thousands of institutions, most of which will employ them for other research as well. Of equal significance, the Food and Drug Administration's regulations for testing pediatric drugs will conform to these guidelines. State legislatures and agencies are also likely to use the regulations as models. The regulations may even affect the law of medical malpractice relating to informed consent.

I hope that the presentations and discussions that follow will find their way into the proceedings of the National Commission.

CHILDREN AS SUBJECTS FOR MEDICAL EXPERIMENTATION

Charles Fried

The debate regarding the use of children as experimental subjects has produced two extreme positions:

1. Children may not be exposed to risks of any sort or degree in the course of medical experimentation except when that risk is necessary to procure a proportionate benefit to that child.

2. Children constitute a discrete population for the purposes of medical therapy. There are diseases that only children have, and there are responses to medical interventions that are peculiar to children. Therefore, children may be enrolled in medical experiments, even those involving some risk but of no benefit to the particular child on that occasion, provided only that the overall social benefit of the experiment outweighs the risk.

Now, as to whether children can be subjected to risks not for their own benefit in the course of medical experimentation, I feel like the Maine farmer who, when asked whether he believed in infant baptism, responded, "Hell, yes, I have seen it done." The fact is, of course, that children entering hospitals and clinics are regularly exposed to an additional venipuncture or x-ray. Children undergoing surgery may be kept under anesthesia 5 or 10 minutes longer to monitor some effect that is not strictly necessary to their treatment. An extra few millimeters of skin may be taken or a small bone chip may be removed for examination during surgery while the child is under anesthesia. Sometimes, in the case of metabolic diseases with clear genetic components, a child-sibling may be asked to undergo blood tests or even intestinal biopsies obtained by the ingestion of a biopsy capsule. In thousands of such instances, it is quite plain that the very small risks run will produce benefits only long after the particular child has ceased to suffer from the disease, if ever.

In other cases, risks of a similar or perhaps slightly more substantial nature are imposed on children with the thought that the information yielded might in fact lead to a remedy in time to help this child. Nevertheless, no candid researcher (or informed consent document) would induce entry into the experiment by representing it as a way of dealing with this patient's particular situation. A justification is found in terms of benefits that are most likely to accrue to others.

These are the types of cases we must consider. I discount the case of the pediatric cancer patient who has failed all standard therapies and is given a hazardous new remedy in the desperate hope that this might be of some help. Whatever the research aims in such a case, the alternatives are so grim that—except when a peaceful end is what is desired by and for the child—anything with the slightest chance of success represents a net expected benefit to the child.

On the other hand, we must certainly include in the difficult, problematic area I am considering a number of double-blind random clinical trials in which children are randomized between a conventional therapy and an experimental therapy, or between an experimental therapy and no therapy at all.

It is quite plain by now that the standard, or what I would call the charmer's technique, for arguing that the random clinical trial does not involve some prejudice to the interests of the particular subject is in fact a phony argument. There is some belief that one of the random alternatives is better. Or the particular subject might have preferences for one of the two alternatives that are not completely taken into account by randomization.

I do not condemn random clinical trials, but I insist that they involve some variation in the treatment of the subject that is not strictly intended for that subject or that occasion, but is introduced in order to procure or to verify knowledge, in order to procure a benefit for others. Therefore, we must consider most randomized trials as examples of problematic research on children. Not necessarily bad research, but the kind of research that is our subject.

Now the standard, what one might call the ancient common law, view of the matter may very well prohibit any experimentation involving children that does not fall under the first extreme view, that whatever risks the child encounters can only be justified in terms of benefits expected to accrue to that child specifically. Indeed, the very purpose of exposing the child to the risk must be to procure the benefit. This standard common law position is derivable from a few common law axioms:

Axiom 1.   No intentional impingement upon the body of another is lawful except with that other person's consent.

Axiom 2.   A minor person is not legally competent to consent, and therefore a minor's consent is not sufficient to make lawful what would be impermissible under axiom 1.

Axiom 3.   The consent of a minor may only be given by a specially authorized person, usually a parent, but possibly a court appointed guardian.

Axiom 4.   A minor's lawful guardian, in giving consent, must do so motivated only by the interests of the minor, and may not use his or her tutelary authority to further his own or some third person's interests.

Therefore, because minors cannot give effective consent to risky medical procedures not designed solely for their benefit, and because their guardians may not consent for them, no medical procedure may proceed without consent, no such experimental procedures may be carried out on minors. It is striking indeed that Professor Ramsey's position is isomorphic with this common law position.

The common law conception was well illustrated by the early kidney transplant cases, in which donor tissue compatibility was much more of an issue than it is now. When minors were involved, surgeons were extremely hesitant to operate upon the donors and court orders were sought. In some early cases courts, acting as guardians in this matter, followed the common law (or Ramsey) theorem and forbade the donations. But this position came under increasing pressure. Cases arose in which plainly the donor very much wished to donate, in which the donor was closely attached (particularly in the case of a twin) to a critically ill brother or sister, in which testimony was produced that the psychological damage to the potential donor of the ill sibling's death would be far worse than any risks involved in the donation. These pleas were heard and the donations were permitted on such showings.

The Farinelli case in Massachusetts is an example of a court moving toward a new doctrine. Common law is, after all, a set of doctrines that evolve in time. The Farinelli case involved the much less hazardous procedure of a bone marrow transplant in an experimental attempt to overcome a fatal blood disease: aplastic anemia. The donation was obviously much less hazardous than a kidney donation (though not without discomforts and risks), but the benefits also were far less palpable. The court, rather than proceeding on the basis that the potential donor would suffer psychological harm if he did not donate, pushed through to the perception that permitting the donation was proper because the donation was a good act, a right act, and therefore the court should authorize it.

The astuteness of this decision deserves attention, because the "psychological harm" ploy for allowing altruistic acts rests on a deep and persistent fallacy that is common to consequentialist rationalizations for a wide range of nonconsequentialist moral judgments. For instance, utilitarians account for the widely held intuition that lying, promise breaking, and harming innocent persons are all wrong by recourse to a feeling or sentiment that these acts make us uncomfortable, guilty, or insecure. Utilitarian authors argue that concern for the well-being of others is based on a sentiment of sympathy, an emotional identification with the sufferings of others such that we feel their suffering as our own. In this way, in doing good to others, we are only seen to be doing good to ourselves after all. Yet few if any of these utilitarian rationalizations work. Either they dissolve into an empty tautology or they fail to account for the variety and power of moral judgments they are meant to cover.

In the end, it is truer to the facts and to our moral intuitions to do the thing the other way around: we abhor the deliberate condemnation of an innocent man because it is a gross injustice; we do not characterize it as a gross injustice because we abhor it. Similarly, we do not help others because their pain makes us uncomfortable, but rather the pain of our fellow beings concerns us because it is right that it should do so. We do not help others because it is gratifying to help others. Rather it is gratifying to help others because it is morally right to help. I would add here that we do not help others so that we may "grow morally." If there is moral education in helping others, it is simply because there may be moral education in doing the right thing. So I would suggest that we not take the easy, and I think somewhat fallacious, way out of these dilemmas. We should confront them directly.

In just the same way, the Farinelli court saw that tissue donations should not be allowed on this ground of some real or supposed psychological benefits accruing to the donor. If there are such benefits, they accrue because the donor is doing the right thing. The donation should be permitted because the donation is right. If the donor feels good about making the donation or would feel bad about not making the donation, these feelings are not the reason for permitting or refusing to forbid the donation. Rather, they are the result of the response to the perception of the moral quality of the donation.

This conception is at least the implicit conception behind the present federal regulations, which do not prohibit experimentation involving children where there are risks not completely justified by reference to the benefits to that child in that case. In November 1973, regulations were proposed dealing specifically with children that would have been considerably more restrictive than current practice. The vehemence of the outcry from the research community blocked their final promulgation. Nevertheless, even these regulations would not have adopted what I have been calling the common law or the Ramsey theorem. Rather, they moved in a direction that may be taken as generally sound, of making the child's own consent much more important. Children who were approaching maturity could consent to experimental procedures even without their guardians' joining in the consent. In the case of less mature children, above the age of 7, I believe, the consent of the child, although not sufficient, is necessary, and only in the case of very young children could the child's consent be dispensed with altogether, under rigid safeguards. For instance, there would have to be some other person standing in the position of guardian. Children who are institutionalized or who do not have natural or adoptive parents could not be used in such experiments. These guidelines never became effective, but I believe many institutions nevertheless are following their spirit. I know the institution on whose review board I sit, the Children's Hospital in Boston, operates very much in the spirit of these guidelines.

This is wise, I think, because these guidelines represent a point of view that is at the convergence of a large number of developing doctrines in the law. The new common law replaces the more wooden old common law theorem. These new doctrines represent what one might call the emancipation of the child. After all, the common law doctrine making the consent of minors ineffective might be subject to a less benign interpretation than that which I have offered. It might be susceptible to the interpretation that the child is in some sense, during minority, the creature of his or her guardian. A variety of recent decisions have affirmed a moral equal status for the rights of children. The principle case, of course, is the Gault decision, which held that children are entitled to the full panoply of rights in juvenile proceedings, and that they cannot be deprived of these rights—the right to counsel, the right to confront accusers, the privilege against self-incrimination—on the grounds that the state in these proceedings is acting in loco parentis. That is to say, children have rights even though a guardian purports to be acting in their best interests and to be better able to further the child's interests if the child's rights are ignored. A variety of decisions stating that minors may obtain abortions and that parental consent may not be made a condition of an abortion represent another convergent thread in this developing strain. Similar decisions have held that children may obtain contraceptive advice and devices if they wish without the consent of their parents. Similarly, a decision holding that a minor cannot be forced to have an abortion because a guardian wishes it comes to the same conclusion from another direction. Finally, one might mention cases dealing with dress codes, hair length rules, and the like, in which it has been held that schools—although in loco parentis—may not exercise such pervasive authority over minors.

The general theme seems to be that, so far as possible, the autonomy of children should not be compromised by those purporting to act in their best interests, any more than the autonomy of mental patients or those accused of crime. If we now apply this developing tendency in common and constitutional law to the subject before us, we see how it differs from and resembles the decided cases. The theme of the decided cases would seem to be that a minor should determine his or her own life-style. Assume that an institutional review board has found that an experiment does not involve undue risk and that, in any case, the risk is justified by the benefits to others. Why should a minor have less autonomy to make the altruistic decision to enter an experiment than to make decisions relating to the use of his or her reproductive functions, education, or exercise of legal rights? It would be ironic indeed if a child were granted greater autonomy in respect to sexual conduct or misconduct or legal rights than about a decision to perform a marginally risky altruistic act.

The trend we notice is surely a sound one. Surely the common law concept of majority and minority never did have much to justify it, and probably catered as much to the authority of parents as to the autonomy and rights of their children. Whether we like it or not, children are asserting greater autonomy at an earlier age. And if this is the trend, should we accept it? Well, this reminds me of Margaret Fuller's statement that she had finally decided to accept the universe, to which the response was, she had better. Well, we had better accept the fact that children have both the opportunity and the determination to exercise more autonomy. All we can do is respond in ways that will make the exercise of that autonomy creative, instructive, and fruitful for the future. To allow children from the age of 11 onward, let us say, to decide whether to participate in reasonable, but somewhat hazardous experimentation would seem to be not a crucial, but a reasonable manifestation of such a program. To put the matter differently, it seems to me to tell the worst of all possible stories, a story favoring self-indulgence and selfishness, to say to young people that they are free to have sex with whom they want, to have or not to have abortions, to wear what clothes they wish and hair of whatever length they wish, but that they may not perform a reasonable and useful act of generosity.

The real difficulty, of course, relates to children before the age of nascent responsibility. I cannot give you the precise age I am talking about, but surely children below the age of 8, 7, 6 years old. I suggest that, to the extent that these children can understand at all what they are doing, they, too, should have some opportunity to make a contribution to medical research. Of course, their consent can never be sufficient. Their parents must also consent, but it must be understood that their parents are consenting to something that is an act of generosity on the part of the child. In this instance, however, one would want to make a much closer connection between that child and the benefit he or she is producing. One would want to make a connection of the sort that requires the research to benefit a close relative, or perhaps those suffering from a disease this child is also suffering from. For there the community of interests is tightly drawn. Indeed, if one considers a disease such as cystic fibrosis or one of the juvenile cancers, it is fairly certain that whatever help the potential subject-child is presently receiving comes itself as the result of similar sacrifices by earlier children.

Now as judgment and understanding recede and we approach true infancy, the old flat-footed common law theorem has much more power. In the case of a baby, not only is the educational and self-determination value totally missing, but the safeguard against abuse and imposition, achieved by making the child's consent a necessary condition, no longer obtains. Without that safeguard, I think one has a right to be concerned. And yet I would not make an absolute of this matter. I would not join the lawsuit, for instance, that has lost so far in California to enjoin the taking of small amounts of blood and the maintenance of doses of harmless medications in children for the purposes of clinical investigation. I hope I will be forgiven the pun if I say that here, too, the maxim should hold de minimis non curet lex.

Now as an inveterate believer in rights, someone who has an allergy to reducing everything to weighing and balancing, someone who believes in moral absolutes, this may seem an unsatisfactory state in which to leave matters. But I do not believe it is so. Certainly in respect to those children who are above the age of infancy, I move in the direction I suggest as much out of a concern for the rights of children as out of a desire to advance medical research. However, in general, I do not see that rights are violated where a minimally risky and useful invasion of the body occurs with the consent of a guardian and at least not against the consent of the subject. In other words, the right I recognize is a right to be free from bodily intrusions *against* consent one has not given, but might have given.

Here I must add a comparison between my view and that which Professor Ramsey set forth before me. The way I would schematize my view is this: First, the basic principle is: do not intentionally impose on a person against that person's will. Second, parents should care for their children. Third, to contribute to others is good. Fourth, it is open to parents as part of their care to enlist their children to do a reasonable and good thing, which as parents they themselves would have done, so long as this is not against the will of the child.

Now Professor Ramsey has a different view, and if we try to locate that difference we locate it in the first and the second of my propositions. It must be that Professor Ramsey has the view that the first premise is not, as I would say, do not intentionally impose on another against that person's will, but rather, do not intentionally impose upon another without that person's consent. If you state it that way, the rest of his argument follows. However, the question is why do it that way, and Ramsey does not tell us why. I propose a different premise, which strikes me as at least as reasonable, and which has to recommend it the fact that it does not lead to what seems a fanatical conclusion. My premise is: do not impose upon another against that person's will. I am prepared to be just as absolute about that as he is about his, but I invite you to consider which of these premises seems to you to be more reasonable. I think it is open to ask, in deciding on the reasonableness of the premise, how reasonable the conclusions are that you draw from that premise. In my view, the conclusions that Ramsey draws from his premise are unreasonable, even though, when stated in the abstract, they may not seem noticeably different from my own. I therefore suggest that my premise is more acceptable.

Then we may differ on the meaning of the proposition that parents should care for their children. Ramsey would draw from this proposition the corollary that a parent who exposes a child to even a minimal risk except solely for that child's own, if you like, selfish benefit is not caring for that child. Once again, stated in that way, the conclusions he draws from that premise flow logically, but one should examine whether that is a premise we should accept. I do not believe any reason was given by Ramsey. What was given was a demonstration that his conclusions follow, if you accept that premise. I would like to suggest that is not a premise we should accept.

In research on children, excesses must be doubly guarded against. However, given justified research, executed in a responsible manner, children can be considered appropriate subjects as long as being part of a research project is not intentionally imposed on them against their will, and as long as participation is a reasonable and good thing that their parents themselves would have done if appropriate.

THE IMPACT OF FEDERAL REGULATIONS GOVERNING EXPERIMENTATION ON MEDICAL MALPRACTICE LAW

Catherine Damme

This chapter discusses the effect of violation of regulations on civil suits for malpractice. To my knowledge, there are no state statutes specifically dealing with experimentation on children. A number of states do have regulations, policies, and even less formalized controls on such research, but they are often applicable only to minors who are institutionalized. The most influential and far reaching code of behavior for experimenters on children may soon be proposed by the National Commission for the Protection of Human Subjects of Biomedical and Behavioral Research. However, the draft document, issued by that organization this month, is not final and, from what I understand from various staffers and members, does not represent a consensus of opinion on the subject. There is wide disagreement, and it would be quite dangerous to speculate as to what the final recommendations will contain.

However, the commission is responsible for developing recommendations that became the regulations that do exist and now apply to experimentation on both adults and minors. Violation of these regulations (and the regulations that may emerge relating to children) results in loss of funds. What this chapter deals with is the impact of violation of these regulations on the violator's civil liability in malpractice suits.

Most such suits probably turn on the issue of informed consent. However, some actions could also arise on other grounds, for instance, from an allegedly faulty risk-benefit determination by an institutional review board under 45 CFR § 46.102(b) (1) of the federal regulations now in force. Because of the very few state regulations that exist in this area, I will direct my remarks to the malpractice issues that might be affected by violation of federal regulation, and concentrate on the question of liability in informed consent suits.

Although I address the existing regulations on informed consent in the experimental context, I feel it is necessary to say a word about the special problems that may be raised by promulgation of regulations specifically applicable to experimentation on children. As Professor Fried has pointed out, the traditional role of the child in informed consent has been enforced passivity. Under common law, the child has been considered incapable of giving legally effective consent, and only parental proxy consent to a procedure for the child's benefit would pass legal muster. However, there has been a steady erosion of the view of the child as a vegetable-like being, incapable of giving consent. Courts and legislatures have moved to free the child from the necessity of gaining parental consent to medical treatment under certain circumstances. Many states allow children to seek treatment for a wide range of conditions, including venereal and other contagious diseases and pregnancy, without parental knowledge or consent. And the United States Supreme Court has affirmed the female minor's right to receive an abortion without parental consent in the recent Danforth decision.

This trend toward recognition of the child's right to decide his or her own fate is continued in the draft recommendations of the National Commission for the Protection of Human Subjects. As I mentioned before, this may bear little resemblance to the final document. However, it is clear that some form of consent from the child will be required under some circumstances. Although the child's consent alone will probably not be sufficient, there is evidence that, in certain situations, the child's objection may be controlling even in the face of parental permission. Of course, the age of the child, the type of experiment, the risk to the child, and the benefit to be derived (both by the child and by others) are factors that will contribute to resolution of a conflict between the child's and the parents' wishes on participation in an experimental therapy.

The necessity of dual consent (from both parent and child) for some experimental protocols and failure to obtain it for others, the coercive influence of the parental decision on the child's decision, and a host of other issues will surely present the courts with complex questions of legal liability in civil actions involving the informed consent issue, should the commission's final recommendations become regulation. However, right now it would be premature to speculate on those actions. What is of more immediate import is the effect of the existing regulations on informed consent actions.

Informed consent cases are usually based on the theory that the physician was negligent in failing to disclose certain information to the patient. The plaintiff/patient must first establish that the defendant/physician owed him or her a duty of care (usually defined by a standard of behavior or standard of care). The plaintiff must then show that the defendant breached the duty of care and that the breach was the proximate cause of his or her injuries. The injured person establishes this causal relationship by showing that, but for the failure of the defendant/physician to transmit necessary information to him, he would not have consented to the procedure. In other words, if the physician had disclosed the information, the patient would have withheld consent.

Of singular importance in informed consent actions is what standard of care is used by the courts in a particular jurisdiction to measure the disclosure practices of a physician. The professional standard is the most prevalent. Under that standard, which is the traditional standard of care in malpractice cases generally, the physician need only disclose information that a reasonable physician in his locale under similar circumstances would disclose. This standard, of course, necessitates the use of expert witnesses—i.e., physicians—to assess whether or not the standard has been breached.

Another standard, which has so far been adopted in about 14 jurisdictions, is the societal standard. Under this relatively new measure, the physician must disclose all information that a patient would deem material to his decision to consent to a procedure. This standard, which obviates the need for an expert witness, is gaining acceptance in more and more jurisdictions. Two variations of the societal standard exist: the social objective standard, in which the jury must decide what information a reasonable patient under those circumstances would find material, and the social subjective standard, in which the jury must decide what information that particular patient with his emotions, phobias, etc., would consider material.

These are the standards that are employed in a traditional informed consent malpractice action, but it is difficult to discern a professional standard of care in experimentation. Some evidence of one emerges in a Texas case, Karp. v. Cooley, in which the plaintiff was the wife of a patient who had died of renal failure after heart surgery, which resulted in an implantation of a mechanical heart, followed shortly thereafter by transplantation of a human heart. Mrs. Karp sued the surgeon who had performed the procedures. She contended, among other things, that he had failed to get proper informed consent for an experimental procedure, implantation of the mechanical heart.

Texas is a "professional standard" state in which a physician need only disclose the risks that a reasonable practitioner under similar circumstances would disclose to a patient. There was evidence that the physician had informed the patient that the mechanical heart pump had not been used in humans, but only in animal experiments. The full results of these experiments were apparently not revealed to the patient. The Fifth Circuit Court of Appeals concluded that an action based on lack of informed consent in an experimental procedure must be measured by the traditional malpractice standard in Texas. Because the plaintiff could not produce expert testimony to demonstrate that the defendant breached his duty to inform the patient of the experimental nature of the artificial heart, the cause of action was dismissed. The defendant was, in effect, in the position of setting his own standard because the procedure had never before been attempted and determination of what his peers would disclose would be purely speculative; he had no peers in this situation.

One might conclude from this case that the professional standard is that the reasonable physician would reveal, at the very least, that the procedure had not been attempted on a human subject. The patient would then know that he had agreed to undergo an experimental therapy.

This professional standard becomes rather confusing if we project it onto a practitioner and an institution covered by the HEW regulations on experimentation. The regulations themselves may seem slightly confusing. Under § 46.102, the institution is first required to obtain "legally effective informed consent." All that is needed in Texas, under Karp v. Cooley, to gain legally effective informed consent is adherence to the professional (and professionally set) standard of disclosure. However, the regulations go on to say that the legally effective informed consent must be obtained "by adequate and appropriate methods in accordance with the provisions of this part."

The elements of informed consent are then defined as:

1. A fair explanation of the procedures to be followed, and their pur-
    poses, including identification of any experimental procedures
2. A description of any attendant discomforts and risks reasonably
    to be expected
3. A description of any benefits reasonably to be expected
4. A disclosure of any appropriate alternative procedures that might
    be advantageous for the subject
5. An offer to answer any inquiries concerning the procedures
6. An instruction that the person is free to withdraw his or her
    consent and to discontinue participation in the project or activity
    at any time without prejudice to the subject.

This definition comes close to the way courts define elements
necessary to the societal standard of disclosure in that a great deal of
information is required to be transmitted to the subject/patient in an
effort to put him in a participatory and controlling role in his consent
decision.

What standard, then, would a court in any state in which
the professional standard is used impose in an informed consent-
experimentation action against a physician covered by the HEW regulations? Although a good deal less than what is required in the HEW
consent definition might be legally effective in a professional standard
state, should the court substitute the higher societal standard and
uphold a cause of action even though testimony shows the defendant/
physician disclosed all that a reasonable practitioner in his community
would have disclosed under similar circumstances?

If a court made such a rating and liability ultimately resulted
because of a breach of an HEW-defined standard, then the question
would become: does that standard replace the professional standard in
all informed consent actions involving experimentation, or does the
professional standard remain viable in cases in which the defendant is
not covered by the regulations?

A very few states have proposed legislative adoption of the HEW
standards for experimentation as state law. Such measures would
surely lessen the confusion that might arise in civil actions when the
court is faced with defining a standard of disclosure, in that state
policy and legislative intent on the standard would be implied in the
statute. Other state departments of public health have adopted the
HEW regulations as statewide policy on experimentation. Although

these actions do not have the force of law, they can be taken as another manifestation of state intent on defining standards of disclosure and would thus have an impact on a court's deliberations on standard setting for disclosure in a civil suit.

Perhaps of more importance than these scattered and disparate state actions is the wide use of the regulations throughout the country as they apply to federally supported research efforts. Because federal funds support the bulk of research and experimentation, the frequent reliance on the informed consent standards may give rise to a national standard of disclosure in civil actions on informed consent in experimentation.

However, the existence of a statutorily implied state standard of disclosure or judicial recognition of a national standard of disclosure may raise questions of evidentiary weight to be given to demonstration of breach of these duties. Similar questions may arise in a state that has maintained the traditional professional standard in malpractice and has not enunciated its policy on experimentation.

Let us return to the previous example of a civil suit commenced in a professional standard state against a physician covered by HEW regulations. We have discussed the possibility of the court adoption of the HEW definition as the standard and rejection of the professional standard (if less rigid). Whichever standard the court employed, could the plaintiff in the civil suit then introduce evidence of the violation of regulations and contend it constituted negligence per se? The vast majority of courts have held that an inexcusable violation of a statute designed to protect the class of person bringing suit is conclusive on the issue of negligence. In other words, introduction of such evidence leads to a finding of negligence per se, and defenses usually available to a defendant are foreclosed under this doctrine. HEW documents on experimentation on children or on human subjects in general, however, are not statutes; they are, in the case of human subjects, administrative regulations, and in the case of children, merely draft recommendations. As to the regulations, the law is less clear on their evidentiary weight. A number of courts have ruled that violation of administrative regulations such as those relating to experimentation on human subjects may be introduced as evidence of negligence, but the final determination is left to the trier of fact (the jury or judge).

All these issues on malpractice actions I have raised will be compounded if and when regulations on experimentation with children are finally promulgated by HEW. And these problems of civil liability cannot be solved by a federal regulatory agency. They will force state courts and perhaps legislatures to take a more active role in controlling experimentation on human subjects. This is only right. The dearth of regulation on the state level is perhaps symptomatic of a lack of interest there and illustrates yet another abdication to a federal entity; but this should not be so, for it is on the state level, the "front line," as it were, that the greatest opportunity for both control and abuse lies.

FEDERAL REGULATIONS
Their Growth and Intent

Martha M. Freeman

The Food and Drug Administration has special cause to be vitally concerned with issues relating to research in children. We appreciate any opportunity to share in an exchange of viewpoints concerning the various dimensions of the problem. The many facets discussed in this forum reflect the complexity of the problem, as well as the challenge to develop a united approach that will assure that the best interests of children themselves will be served, both collectively and as individuals.

It is the position of the FDA, based upon the recommendations of scientific experts, that carefully defined drug research in children is essential for assuring the availability of safe and effective therapeutic agents for their use. We feel that this goal is consistent with the objective of the Department of Health, Education, and Welfare to improve the nation's health through research, while protecting the rights of those who participate in that research as subjects.

The evolution of regulatory philosophy over the past decade can best be understood from the perspective of legislative history, particularly as it pertains to the "therapeutic orphan" situation. My comments in that regard of course overlap, but also complement earlier discussions.

The Food, Drug, and Cosmetic Act (*1*) requires that drugs be proved safe and effective for each indication and condition of use specified on the labeling, commonly called the package insert. It states that such proof must consist of substantial evidence, based upon adequate and well-controlled clinical investigations performed by qualified experts. The regulations developed by the FDA to administer this law stipulate that a drug must be investigated for each disease condition and under all conditions of use recommended in the labeling such as the dosage level, duration of treatment, and patient populations for whom the drug is intended. Additionally, appropriate warning information must be provided regarding situations in which use is proscribed. Obviously, the law is intended to insure adequate labeling information to enable the physician to administer the drug safely and effectively.

Ironically, labeling for approximately three-quarters of prescription drugs today denies to children the intended protection, either by failing to provide information on pediatric dosage or by a disclaimer that use in children is not recommended because studies in this age group were not performed or were inadequate; the so-called therapeutic orphan clause. This term was coined by Dr. Harry Shirkey, a pediatric pharmacologist, to highlight the plight of sick children in need of therapy for whom no drugs are labeled (2).

Although the law does not prohibit a physician from administering a marketed drug in a manner differing from that specified in the labeling, litigation has resulted on occasion from such use. Therefore, a doctor who undertakes the treatment of sick children may face the choice of either risking liability for nonapproved use and arbitrary fractionation of the adult dose or denying his patient the benefit of drugs known to be effective in treating adults with the same illness.

This dilemma exists because of a legal technicality; if pharmaceutical manufacturers choose not to perform studies that would enable them to specify a pediatric indication or dosage in the label, the statutory requirement for "substantial evidence" derived from pediatric investigation does not apply, consequently, the drug is not studied in children. This paradox is all the more poignant in view of the fact that the present law evolved primarily in response to public demand for increased protection of children from unsafe drugs in the wake of therapeutic disasters. For example, in 1938 preclearance of drugs for safety was mandated by Congress after the elixir of sulfanilamide episode in which more than 100 people died, many of whom were children. The drug law amendments of 1962 were enacted after the thalidomide tragedy in Europe, and not only required that drugs be precleared for effectiveness as well as safety, but also directed the FDA to monitor the use of investigational drugs from the time of their initial introduction into humans until approval for marketing.

The FDA has long deplored the shortage of adequately labeled drugs for the treatment of children, and has participated actively in the joint efforts of academia, industry, and government to explore the causes and to find solutions. One of the two major causative factors identified, a limitation of national resources in terms of qualified pediatric pharmacologists and facilities, is beyond the scope of this symposium and of FDA statutory responsibility. The second factor is at the heart of the present discussions: the increasing public concern over ethical issues, which has led to the increasing reluctance of drug manufacturers and investigators to undertake drug studies in children.

The need for ethical guidelines to protect drug consumers of all ages was underscored in 1975 by Casper Weinberger, then Secretary of Health, Education, and Welfare: "There is no way to abide by the Harrison-Kefauver Act of 1962, as it applies to drugs in children, without first having a clear mandate on the ethical issues of testing drugs on children as subjects. As Secretary of HEW, I am on the horns of a dilemma. I am responsible for effectively promulgating the Food and Drug Law. I must certify that [the] FDA is complying with the law. Yet I am prevented from validating that in the absence of clear ethical guidelines concerning the issue of informed consent among infants and children involved in drug trials" (3).

The FDA's commitment to alleviating the inequities in the application of the law is a matter of public record. In 1972, Dr. Charles Edwards (then commissioner) told the American Academy of Pediatrics, "It is not a question of whether drugs should be studied in children, but rather when, how, in whom, and under what circumstances. . . . I am committed to this effort and to the goal of advancing the New Drug Application (NDA) approval process toward the ideal where any new drug with a potential for use in children is tested for that purpose and approved for that purpose at the same time that the drug is approved for adults" (4). Even earlier, in 1970, Dr. Marion Finkel (then deputy director of the Bureau of Drugs) advised conference participants,

> "We feel that this [therapeutic orphan] situation requires correction when feasible. . . . Accordingly, we are adopting the policy that an NDA for a drug that would have considerable therapeutic utility in children and will be used by the practicing physician in the absence of investigational studies in children will not be approved unless the necessary studies are performed" (5).

Full implementation of this policy has been delayed pending resolution of the ethical issues in the national forum. In 1973, the secretary issued proposed policy and draft regulations concerning the protection of human subjects of research supported by the department, including both general considerations and those applicable to certain groups with impaired ability to give informed consent. In this context, the clearly stated rationale regarding research in children deserves special attention: "Children have generally been considered inappropriate subjects for many research activities because of their inability to give informed consent. There are certain circumstances which not only justify, but even require, their participation. Children do differ from adults in their physiologic responses, both to drugs and to disease; if the health of the nation is to be improved, it is necessary to know the nature and extent of these differences, and to have a full understanding of normal patterns of growth and development. Studies of normal physiology and behavior can also provide significant benefits to children suffering from disease; children are the only subjects from whom these data can be obtained. Furthermore, there are diseases which cannot be induced in laboratory animals, and occur only rarely, if at all, in human adults. In such cases, children are the only subjects in whom the disease process and possible modes of therapy can be studied" (6). Publication of the final regulations has been postponed until the recommendations are available from the National Commission for the Protection of Human Subjects of Biomedical and Behavioral Research. This commission was established by congressional mandate in 1974 to study and identify the basic ethical principles underlying the conduct of biomedical and behavioral research in human subjects, and to advise Congress and the HEW Secretary regarding the protection of human subjects (7). It is anticipated that the recommendations of the commission will establish definitive public policy that will be implemented through departmental and agency regulations.

While the issue of nontherapeutic research in children awaits resolution at this high level, the FDA has endorsed and will be guided by the recommendations of the American Academy of Pediatrics (AAP) regarding therapeutic research, as stated in 1969:

> "The great need for information regarding the effects of drugs, especially in very young infants, can be met by carefully conducted tests of new drugs on ill children who may be expected to benefit from the drug. The design, recording and reporting of such studies is in the interest of the profession, the drug industry, and most importantly the children" (8).

Risks will be minimized by requiring prior data from adults to define safety, effectiveness, and disposition of the drug within the body (recognizing that there may be some differences in drug metabolism in children), and by initiating studies in older children, proceeding cautiously to infants as safety permits. Peer review, valid consent, and the use of methodology consistent with the size of the patients are inherent requirements for such studies. In order to stimulate the necessary studies and to assure their scientific validity and ethical acceptability, the FDA sought contractual assistance from the AAP through its Committee on Drugs for the development of guidelines for testing drugs in children. To date they have produced, through consultation with FDA advisory committees, outside experts in law and science, and liaison contacts with the National Commission, comprehensive General Guidelines for the Evaluation of Drugs to Be Approved for Use During Pregnancy and for Treatment of Infants and Children; a guideline detailing ethical considerations to be observed in performing drug studies in children; and eight guidelines for studying specific classes of drugs in children. After review by appropriate FDA advisory committees and final approval within the Bureau of Drugs, they will be released for general use by manufacturers and investigators. It is our hope and expectation that the authoritative origin and endorsement of these guidelines by the AAP will help overcome public concern and professional reluctance regarding the performance of drug studies in children.

Until now, the performance of pediatric studies has been on an ad hoc basis: voluntarily undertaken by manufacturers (primarily the case with antibiotics) or by agreement between the FDA and the manufacturer. On occasion, we have requested postmarketing studies in children after approval for marketing in adults, and recently several new drug applications were approved contingent upon the agreement that pediatric studies would be completed in the postmarketing phase.

It is now our intent to issue in the near future a policy statement and draft regulations to require pediatric studies as a condition for the marketing of all new drugs that either promise an important therapeutic advantage over those already available for use in children or will be widely used in children because of their applicability or special features, such as dosage form or delivery system. Drugs that are redundant within a class or that offer no particular advantage will not require testing, but they must be clearly labeled to the effect that they have not been studied in children.

Dr. Marion J. Finkel has developed and publicized criteria for determining which drugs under investigation will require pediatric data and whether the necessary studies should be completed before marketing or in the postmarketing phase (9).

Pediatric studies should be completed before marketing for: a) drugs representing major therapeutic advances and likely to be used in children; b) drugs not representing major advances, but likely to be used widely in children because of their novelty, e.g., the first new anti-inflammatory agent in 9 years, or their applicability, e.g., a drug for pinworm or acute leukemia.

Pediatric studies should be completed after marketing for drugs that represent some advantage over other available drugs and are likely to be used in children to a significant extent, but not so widely as in b above.

Pediatric studies should not be required for: a) drugs likely to have insignificant use in children or to be unnecessary; b) drugs that have no discernible advantage over other available drugs for use in children; c) drugs for which efficacy and safety in children would be expected to be similar in children as in adults, e.g., a topical, relatively nonabsorbable antifungal agent.

By applying these criteria in the early stages of drug development, a pharmaceutical manufacturer will be able to plan such studies as part of the total investigation and not have to add them as a costly afterthought when the investigation is otherwise complete. Flexibility will be allowed in applying the criteria, however, because this regulation is not intended to delay the availability of significant new drugs for adult patients. For example, a new drug considered to be a major therapeutic advance in the management of hypertensive emergencies would not be kept off the market for adult use until testing could be completed in children, in view of the small number of children who would require such therapy and would therefore be appropriate test subjects. Final decisions in identifying drugs for pediatric studies will be arrived at in consultation with the manufacturers and expert advisers.

In order to assess the likely impact of this policy upon allegedly limited resources, these criteria were applied retrospectively to the list of 77 significant new drugs approved during the past 5 years. This analysis revealed that approximately one-third would require completion of pediatric studies in the premarketing and one-sixth in the postmarketing phase. This would add approximately two or three new drugs per year requiring premarketing pediatric data, and approximately two new drugs per year requiring postmarketing pediatric data beyond those already being studied on an ad hoc basis. We trust that available facilities will accommodate this additional requirement, and that additional training and testing facilities will be established to facilitate continued progress in meeting children's therapeutic needs.

In closing, I would like to say that this proposed regulation may well serve as the proving ground for the emerging accommodation of conflicting values achieved through forums such as this, and as the final common pathway for translating into action the resulting policy that has been tempered by public concern. It is our hope and expectation that it may represent a regulatory milestone in assuring children the same safeguards mandated for adults regarding the safety and effectiveness of marketed drugs.

ACKNOWLEDGMENT

I am grateful to Dr. Marion J. Finkel, Associate Director for New Drug Evaluation, Bureau of Drugs, FDA, for her helpful comments in the organization and preparation of this manuscript.

REFERENCES

1. Public Law 87-871 Oct. 10, 1962. Food, Drug, and Cosmetic Act (Drug Amendments of 1962).
2. Shirkey, H. 1968. Therapeutic orphans. (Editorial comment). J. Pediatr. 72:119–120.
3. Weinberger, C. W. 1972. Experiments and research with humans: values in conflict. Keynote Address at NAS Forum, February 19, 1975.
4. Edwards, C. C. 1972. Keynote Address to American Academy of Pediatrics, October 16.
5. Finkel, M. J. 1970. Investigational and new drugs: what does the FDA expect? University of Wisconsin IND-NDA Conference October 4–7, (FDA Papers, November 1970).
6. Federal Register. Nov. 16, 1973. 38:31738–31749.
7. Public Law 93-348, National Research Act, July 12, 1974.
8. AAP Committee on Drugs, Drug Testing in Children. 1969. FDA regulations. Pediatrics 43:463–464.
9. Finkel, M. J. 1976. Drug Studies in Children. Am. Soc. Clin. Pharm. Ther. March 18.

THE FEDERAL GOVERNMENT AND POLICY DECISIONS INVOLVING CHILDREN

Floyd A. Norman

Each speaker has taken liberties with his or her subject. That is progressive, and I think not inappropriate. I was asked to reveal all I dared about the federal government and health as it relates to children. As you know, my return trip would be impossible if I were to do that. Therefore, I will have to talk a bit in riddles. Most of you have had experience with the federal government and will understand what I say. Some things I can state outright. I was also asked to talk about the political perspective. I know very little about politics and, because of the Hatch act, all I do is read the paper.

Sometimes I think the federal government is a very impotent dragon, instead of a powerful one. Yet it could be powerful. It is a maze of agencies. Those of us who work fulltime there at full salary do not understand it, cannot comprehend it, cannot keep up with it. It is hard to do justice to the complexities in 5 or 10 minutes. But is there a national health policy for children and is there a need for it? That is the bait that made me participate.

In this chapter a few facts are given and then discussed. At least 58 pieces of legislation might be identified as relating to the health of mothers and children. For the purposes of this discussion, maternal and child health care are not separated. If one thinks infants or fetuses are of value (and there is some question in our society today), one would not argue with that grouping. The federal establishment alone manages 106 programs.

The total amount of money assigned to this broad array of child, maternal, and infant health programs is $32.4 billion. That should buy quite a lot of something. One can identify some of it pretty well. Over $5 billion goes into the food stamp program, for example. The best kind of estimate you can do with good armchair bureaucracy suggests that $12.6 billion affects the health of mothers and children. Only about $2.2 billion of these federal funds support personal health services for children. The Social Security Administration employs many people who spend considerable time doing things with figures. They come out a little bit different, but not too much. They calculate maternal and child health services on a pay-out basis. The figure they obtain is about $15.4 billion per year. Of this, $2.45 billion comes from federal funds, $1.3 billion from state and local, and $11.7 billion from private sources. The average cost of health care for one child for a year is probably over $200. That figure comes from the Department of Defense, CHAMPUS, and other sources. It is not current nor completely valid, but if it is roughly true, at least $1 billion more is needed to provide adequate child, infant, and maternal health care services.

A lot of other efforts have been going on, and I will not belabor them too much: Medicaid and the early periodic screening effort, which has certainly taken a long time to get off to a rather miserable and much criticized start. There were some good elements, some controversial elements, and great difficulties in implementation. In nutrition and community mental health programs where the patient load now is about one-quarter children, we find many other sources of services. However, in spite of many significant interventions from the federal bureaucracy, state health departments, categorical service programs, financial aid programs for some of the poor, and specific efforts to attack special disease problems, many mothers and children are still denied access to comprehensive primary care by financial and organizational obstacles. I would like to focus on two of these.

The first is a barrier of utilization. Now that we may have a new Assistant Secretary for Health, we will be at least pediatrically and primary health care service oriented. We should be able to do a bit better in this regard than we have done the last 2 years. I would like to quote a draft plan, entitled "A Proposal for New Federal Leadership in Child and Maternal Health Care in the United States," which will remain in draft form until the new Assistant Secretary for Health reviews it.

When we look at the barriers of utilization, there are many. The dollars already in the health care system are often inefficiently used.

The result is an inadequate system with little public support for costly additions. To cite the figures I stated previously: according to the draft, "Dividing the $15.4 billion spent in 1975 on personal health services for children by the 17.5 million children under the age of 19, the use of per capita expenditures is $218 per child." This would be quite a large resource, if it were properly utilized.

The next is a barrier of organization. Another passage from the draft reads:

> The large number of Federal child health programs scattered throughout the government combined with a lack of clear over-all direction results in confusion, duplication, and fragmentation to the detriment of child health. In spite of the multiplication of programs ... the numerous agencies that are responsible for care of part of the child or the health care system of each known disease, none are charged with seeing that every child has access to care, or for making plans for the care of those who are going without. The multiple and fragmented array of programs makes it nearly impossible for the Federal Government to impose any real accountability for the use of public funds, or for the collection of the kind of data necessary for effective planning.

I know that those of you who are not employed by the federal government would probably like to see the federal government issue a direct statement such as this.

Maybe there really should not be quite all of the hopelessness and despair I am revealing. A neighboring state, Arkansas, although it is close to the bottom of many demographic and economic indices, is one of the most progressive states in terms of health care, far more progressive than the state in which we are now meeting. The ability of its health officials to take ideas and convert them into some kind of coordinated effort and attempt to implement them is remarkable. We are working with them to see what they can do with the myriad of programs. Twelve organizations are involved, the Arkansas State Health Department being central. There are 132 programs, 97 of which are considered public and 35 private. Many people involved in the private practice of medicine do not belong in any category. This effort has not progressed very far yet; it is difficult. It is nice to get letters of commitment to each other, but action is an entirely different matter.

It is difficult to convert knowledge and resources into the improvement of health. Otherwise, we would not have institutions and buildings and Saturday conferences such as this. I know it, you know it, and I will not belabor it. There is hope, there is some progress in some areas. Yet I spent much of the past week reviewing the 244 pages of the Forward Plan of the Alcohol, Drug Abuse, and Mental Health Administration, the umbrella agency over the three institutes. It would not be worth your time to hear a long tirade about the inadequacies, the lack of any coordination of effort, the institutes' absolute rigid insistence on independence and noncooperation, even in their research areas. They badly need to share some clinical beds for intramural research (and might get them if they would share), but they will do without rather than be tainted. They have so many common projects, so many common professional needs. The same clients they vie for, they argue over whether to classify as one or another substance abuser. It is ridiculous. And you, we, the taxpayers permit this to happen. It is atrocious and it should be corrected.

What can we really do about this situation? In order to get attention for a program, a need, or a new treatment in this nation, one often goes to the federal government, believing that we have a national conscience, a national value system. Almost all I heard in this conference was concerned with drugs and interventions. I did not hear about the right children have to learn some other basic facts of life, such as how to live together, what to eat to be reasonably healthy, what limits to set. Children have many other rights beyond the right to have or not to have a safe drug.

In Congress there are four primary health Senate Committees, four House Committees, and 28 secondary Senate and House Committees or Subcommittees, each of which has a very strong sense of possession, client relationship, and constituency response. The staff of a committee may say, "You did not write that regulation the way we thought it to be; change it this way," as you attempt to interpret what the law says. And the staff of the committee monitors your interpretation down to the last detail. This is the kind of situation that citizens must be made to understand. They must acquire the same broad view, as they present their particular attitudes, knowledge, and facts to the committees, that they expect Congress itself to have. Otherwise, they help create the narrow programs we now have. I will not take time to critique the Department of Health, Education, and Welfare. It has its own problems with implementation of programs. But sometimes, with what is available in the law, it does a fairly good job. Seven years ago when I entered the government, I would not have said that. Now I feel there is more accountability, more measurement of outcome. There is real attention to management by objectives, and some people are beginning to understand some elements of a system. A manpower management program delineates times and measurable productivity indices. These efforts can all be thwarted, the game can be played many ways, but in the years I have observed HEW, there have been some basic improvements. There must be laws and these laws must be followed, and some give HEW some difficult mandates. All who are interested in the health and welfare of mothers and children should band together, not just for the mentally retarded or any other single group, but for all mothers and children. We must stimulate a demand, as we have in the energy crisis, for a congressional select committee to develop cohesive legislation that would make possible more comprehensive services for children. We are wasting so much of our energy and so many of our professionals at the present time.

It is disappointing to see the limits of the Forward Plan for 1979–1983 for ADAMHA. It does not begin to cope with some of the fascinating new information on families, interpersonal communications, feelings, value systems, worth of the individual, and the many new kinds of prevention and understanding of the healthy family. It is so tremendously lacking! The base, the root of the problems, are ignored while we treat and diagnose and treat the symptoms through-out life. It is immature of us to accept that, and we must not continue to do so.

THE INTEGRATION OF THE PROBLEM

FIVE CENTRAL CONCERNS IN RESEARCH ON CHILDREN
Summarizing Dialogue and Adversity

Robert J. Comiskey

When the planning committee for this conference met a few months ago, we decided to use two central criteria for selecting topics and speakers. The first was that the program should be multidisciplinary, i.e., it should encompass the medical, ethical, and legal aspects of this issue. We wanted to avoid one-dimensionality, as there was a common recognition that a one-dimensional approach to any issue usually leads up blind alleys and blocks constructive dialogue with those in related areas. Second, we hoped that within the medical, ethical, and legal communities a variety of approaches would be apparent so as to present the opportunity for lively discussion.

I believe that our two criteria have been met and the objective of this conference, to provide a forum for public discussion of the issues in research on children, has been accomplished. Throughout the last 2 days these issues have been discussed by representatives of the medical, ethical, and legal communities, and we have seen differing approaches to these issues within each of the communities. The need for research on children has been highlighted by those persons directly engaged in working with children in medical practice. The ethical issues surfacing in our reflection on this need have been developed by those addressing these concerns. Finally, the codification of the medical and ethical concerns, which is one of the responsibilities of the law, has been discussed by those representing the legal profession.

In any conference of this type and duration, one would expect only to touch the surface of the issues. This conference, however, seems to me to have progressed very quickly to the heart of the matter and begin the discussion where others have ended. I think that the breadth and depth of our participants served as a catalyst in the movement from peripheral issues to central concerns. Each of them has brought a wealth of reflective experience and contributed to the common good of the whole conference.

It is my task to bring this conference to a close. It is not possible in my short time remaining to highlight all the fine points made by our participants, but I would like to briefly review some of the more central points. Five central concerns seemed most important in the minds of our speakers, as reference was made to them frequently both in their prepared remarks and in the subsequent discussions.

First, there was a common recognition of the need to analyze carefully the risk-benefit ratio for the children involved in research so as to insure that the risks were far outweighed by the net benefits both for the child involved as subject and for others. The difficulties in providing an adequate analysis of this ratio were singled out in the discussions. Inevitably, these discussions led to further reflection on the question of informed consent.

Discussion of this second concern, informed consent, stressed the importance of determining the meaning of such consent, as well as the problems involved in obtaining it from children or their parental or legal guardians. The exchange between Drs. Ramsey and Fried was particularly significant here. Dr. Ramsey argued that nontherapeutic research on children ought never to be done, as it is impossible to obtain the child's consent. Dr. Fried, on the other hand, argued that, although one ought never to do anything against another person's consent, one could conduct certain forms of nontherapeutic research without that person's consent if the benefits were high and the risks minimal. The consent question remains one of the most widely debated issues in children's research today.

The problem of obtaining consent from a child moved the discussion to questions of child development. Drs. John Holt and Jerome Berryman provided the participants with valuable data on childhood development, citing the similarities and dissimilarities between children and adults. Dr. Kenneth Vaux contributed an important dimension by developing the moral and spirtual aspects of the interaction between children and parents.

A third concern addressed the need for adequate research design. Clearly defined variables, sound hypotheses, consistent methodologies, and a proper selection of research subjects, based on the principles of justice and fairness, were carefully spelled out by the members representing the medical profession, Drs. Sutow, Sullivan, van Eys, Bartholome, and Howell. Discussion frequently centered on whether or not there really was a need for nontherapeutic research on children and the value of double-blind experiments and randomized studies. A fruitful exchange took place between Dr. Freeman, representing the FDA view, and other participants, who raised questions on particular problems associated with such views.

A fourth concern centered on the requirement for forms of social control whereby research proposals could be adequately reviewed and evaluated, either by local institutional review boards or by other existing review boards. Public policy decisions at the federal, state, and local levels become crucial here. The remarks of Drs. Freeman and Norman helped all to understand the problems in formulating and implementing public policy. In addition, Ms. Damme elucidated some of the legal issues that arise when lawmakers attempt to set up legislation regulating research on children. She pointed out that the movement today seems to be away from viewing children as passive participants and toward seeing them as partners with their parents in such research. Dual consent has become a central issue.

The fifth concern focused on the question of adequate compensation for injured research subjects. Although the other four areas of concern are found in all the major medical codes, this one has only begun to be discussed at any great length in recent times. Many commentators advocate such compensation, but point out that the problems associated with developing procedures for equitable compensation are great. However, some attempts are being made to resolve the difficulties. At least one comprehensive study under the direction of an interagency HEW task force is tackling this issue. I am sure we shall see more on this topic in the future as the implications of many of the principles of justice found in our codes are applied to this concern as well.

Each of these concerns was amplified and developed by our participants. Hence, there is no need here to elaborate upon them further. I hope these presentations will be read thoroughly and their contents shared with others interested in the past, present, and future issues of research on children. All participants deserve thanks for the interest and concern shown by their presence and comments during these sessions. I hope we will be able to continue these discussions in the near future.

EPILOGUE

THE PROBLEMS OF ETHICAL RESEARCH AND THE PROBLEMS WITH BEING A CHILD

Jan van Eys

Throughout all the discussions on the ethics of research on children, necessitated because of the medical insistence that such research is needed, there is an underlying axiom that children are not just small adults. However, different people place different emphasis on that axiom. The medical imperative for research stems from the physiological uniqueness of children, whereas the intuitive caution in executing the research stems from their psychological uniqueness. We have, therefore, the makings of a classic misunderstanding: medicine and ethics are not debating the same issues. Even in this workshop, many times the common denominator, the child, was missing. Decision making and policy setting are almost always done by adults for adults on adult concepts, even when allegedly for the benefit of children.

Being a child is difficult. The world belongs to the grown-ups. But these grown-ups do not truly like children, even though they will not often admit it. We will, on the whole, protect a child from deliberately inflicted harm. We are sad when adult afflictions burden a child, regardless of whether such afflictions are physical or mental. But protecting children from harm does not mean accepting children for what they are. In fact, it often establishes a minority status for the children. They are a minority that is tolerated by the majority, but very much controlled and subjugated.

There are, indeed, problems with being a child. Children are unformed beings. They must pass through stages of development to understand the causality that governs our world, our physical laws as well as our human interactions. There are times in children's development when certain complicated accomplishments of the human genius are beyond their cognitive skills. However, there is no child-adult dichotomy. Some accomplishments of civilization that very much shape our lives are fundamentally beyond the grasp of all except the most gifted adults.

Because children still have potential that adults no longer perceive in themselves, they can become threatening to adults, and assertions of adult superiority need to be made very frequently. This magnifies the dependant role of the child. It even generates an endearing position. Children are a protected minority never to be absorbed into the majority as equal persons.

Yet children have a task in society. They must be instilled with sufficient knowledge and wisdom to be able to change what needs changing. When the security of adults is at risk, such teaching is rare. Few adults acknowledge the wisdom of the German poet Heinrich Heine, who said, "You learn more from your children than they learn from you. You teach them a world that was, and they teach you a world that will be."

Research on children brings feelings into sharper focus than almost any other issue surrounding children in our society. Much has been said about the ethics of such research, but the discussion is often philosophical and divorced from the living, suffering children involved. Research is a way of life for dedicated scientist-physicians. The urge to ask questions and the art of obtaining logical answers is not part of a job, not even the hallmark of a profession. There is a beauty in good research that can be admired; it can even be intoxicating. The medical imperative is there, but the questions asked are broad and sweeping. They must be, even when the disease in a single patient is studied intensively and in detail.

The ethical basis of research on children and the principles of informed consent form the measure against which physicians should judge their sensitivity to the rights of their patients. But an ethical system, when it is discussed in order to arrive at internal logic and consistency, may become an end in itself. It can be debated, honed to the sharpness of a cutting logic that removes motives and feelings as bases of the researcher's fiat. The view of the child in that process is that held by society now. The research is conducted in our society by western norms of ethics and law. Such norms are idealized, to be sure, but they are not outside our American culture. The child is the protected minority, unable to participate in this ethics debate.

Debates about the issues of proxy consent, the common good as a justification for research and motivation to participate, and societal obligations to recognize the fruits of research and compensate for the time and effort expended are all necessary. Arguments can be cogent or poor, as in any debate in which reasoning and logic are the weapons. But ultimately there is the encounter between researcher and child in which a decision must be made. The decision can be one of three basic types: First, research on the child must be a priori rejected, as is research on any other "incompetent" minority. Second, the subordinate minority status must be rejected as a basis of judgment. Finally, some compromise between these extremes might be found with special protection for the children. Much of the groping in ethics is an attempt to find guidelines for the last course.

There is something missing in all of this. Researchers and ethicists act toward the child-subjects as parents toward their offspring. But much parental behavior is destructive, overbearing, repressive, and self-serving. There is eternal conflict in many homes between parents and children. Parents view their children as irresponsible rebels; children see their parents as coercive and arbitrary authoritarians. They do not usually argue about the same aspects of the problem at hand, much as the researcher, the ethicist, and the child-research subject view the questions from entirely different vantage points.

Not long ago a book was published, entitled *Liberated Parents, Liberated Children (1)*, in which the practical applications of the concepts of Dr. Haim Ginott were discussed. The basic tenet was that parents can avoid much conflict by treating their children with the dignity any person deserves. There should be a book entitled *Liberated Researchers, Liberated Children*. If the problem of research on children were approached by allowing children the dignity of being the equal partner-participants adults would be, much of the constraint researchers feel would be gone. Many frustrations among researchers are the consequence of attitudes about what a child is. To treat the child with dignity would remove many barriers. The ethical dilemma of "I know I must do this research; the question is too important to leave unanswered" versus "I am not sure I can subject a child to this research" is a consequence of the usual concept of "child." To accept the child as a person worthy of being treated with dignity would liberate the researcher as well as the child. Informed consent is only a small part of this. To treat a person with dignity implies informed consent; there is no other way. It implies informed consent as Holt defines it: to inform, and then to allow "yes" or "no" as equally acceptable answers. But to treat someone with dignity goes immeasurably further. It allows the acceptance of gifts from the child, yet it will not tolerate undeserved praise by the child.

We do not even approach adults in such a manner, but at least with them we catch ourselves transgressing societal norms. Children are not generally accorded the status of persons. They are accepted as human, but personhood, and all the rights, privileges, and dignity pertaining thereto, is not bestowed until much later. This creates our personal difficulties when they are dying (2), and it colors our attitudes toward research on them.

All the contributions to this workshop were pertinent and vital for an understanding of the problem as it now exists, but in many the child was missing. I plea for liberated researchers and liberated children; the problem will then attain an entirely different perspective.

REFERENCES

1. Farber, A., and Mazlish, E. 1975. Liberated Parents, Liberated Children. Avon Books, New York.
2. van Eys, J. Caring for the child who might die. In: D. Barton (ed.), Caring for the Dying. The Williams & Wilkins Company, Baltimore. In press.

Index

Amino acids, levels of, in children, 34
Aplasia, pure red cell, research on, 48
Arkansas, health care in, 135

Benefits to research subject, 74

Causality, types of, defined by Piaget, 91–94
Children
    dignity of, 149–150
    problems with being, 147–150
    rights of, 1–16
        to informed, consent, 5–16
    as subjects for medical experimentation, 107–115
    as therapeutic orphans, 27–31
Communication, interstage, 89–91
Consent
    informed, right of children to, 5–16
    proxy, 70–74
        debates on, 149

Donne, John, 77–78
Drugs, disclaimers and failure to make dosage recommendations for children, by manufacturers of, 28–30

Ethics
    of human as experimental animal, 39–51
    problems of, 147–150
    of research on children
        discussing of, 85–101
        an eclectic view, 87–89
Etiology, clinical research into, 47
Experimentation: *see* Research

Farinelli case, 109–111
Federal government and policy decisions involving children, 133–137
Federal regulations on experimentation
    growth and intent of, 125–131
    impact on malpractice law, 117–123
Food and Drug Administration, 125–129
Food, Drug, and Cosmetic Act, 125–126
Forward Plan of the Alcohol, Drug Abuse, and Mental Health Administration, 135–137

Gault decision, 111–112
Genetics, importance of research on children from viewpoint of, 33–38
Glucose-6-phosphate dehydrogenase deficiency, research in, 45

Hunter syndrome, research on children with, 37
Hypothyroidism, screening tests for, 36

Imperative
    medical, 17–51
    research, 69–70
Informed consent, right of children to, 5–16

Law
    common, on medical experimen-
        tation on children,
        108–109
    malpractice, impact of federal
        regulations governing ex-
        perimentation on,
        117–123
Lazarus syndrome, 77–84
Legal constraints on research on
        children, 103–137
Leukemia, research on, 48
Lewis, C. S., 83–84

Mucopolysaccharidoses, research on
        children with, 36–37
Myeloma, multiple, research on, 48

National Commission for the Pro-
        tection of Human Subjects
        of Biomedical and Behav-
        ioral Research, 117–118,
        128
Normal data, problem of, in child-
        ren, 33–34

Osteosarcoma, therapeutic research
        in management of, 23–25

Parables of Jesus, use of, to com-
        municate with children
        about research on them,
        97–100
Pathophysiology, clinical research
        into, 47
Pediatrician, definition of, 27
Pharmacology, pediatric, need to
        expand, 27–31
Phenylketonuria, screening tests
        for, 35–36
Piaget, Jean, 89–93
Proxy consent, 70–74
    debates on, 149
Pyruvate kinase deficiency, research
        in, 47

Research
    clinical, need for, 40–43
    context of, 49–50
    ethical, problems of, 147–150
    good clinical, 43–49
        questions to be asked in,
            47–48
    guidelines of researcher-subject
            relation, 40
    on children
        central concerns in, 141–143
        central themes in the debate
            on, 69–76
        ethical dimensions of, 57–68
        importance of, from geneti-
            cist's viewpoint, 33–38
        legal dimensions of, 105
        medical dimensions of,
            19–20
        moral and spiritual aspects of,
            55–56
    therapeutic, as necessary mode
            of management, 21–26
    trivial, 44–45
Rights of child, 1–16
    to informed consent, 5–16
Risk, minimal, from research,
        59–60

Screening tests in children, 35–36
Societal constraints on research on
        children, 103–137

Therapy, clinical research on, 48

Wilms' tumor, therapeutic research
        in management of, 21–23